Safeguard Your Hard-Earned Savings

By

Ken Stern

CAREER PRESS
3 Tice Road
P.O. Box 687
Franklin Lakes, NJ 07417
1-800-CAREER-1
201-848-0310 (NJ and outside U.S.)
FAX: 201-848-1727

SAFEGUARD YOUR HARD-EARNED SAVINGS

ISBN 1-56414-173-X, $11.99

Cover design by The Gottry Communications Group, Inc.

Printed in the U.S.A. by Book-mart Press

To order this title by mail, please include price as noted above, $2.50 handling per order, and $1.00 for each book ordered. Send to: Career Press, Inc., 3 Tice Road., P.O. Box 687, Franklin Lakes, NJ 07417.

Or call toll-free 1-800-CAREER-1 (Canada: 201-848-0310) to order using VISA or MasterCard, or for further information on books from Career Press.

Library of Congress Cataloging-in-Publication Data

Stern, Ken, 1965-
    Safeguard your hard-earned savings / by Ken Stern.
       p.   cm.
    Includes index.
    ISBN 1-56414-173-X : $11.99
    1. Aged--Finance, Personal. 2. Retirement--United States--Planning.
3. Saving and investment. 4. Retirement communities--United States.
5. Social security. 6. Medicare. I. Title.
HG179.S5586   1995
332.024--dc20
                                                                    94-46670
                                                                       CIP

Acknowledgments

This book could not have been completed without the help of some very special people. First and foremost, my mother, who taught me more than she knows. My father, who always comes up with more after I think I have milked all his knowledge. My brother and sister—their life force is enough to make anyone smile and to energize me when no one else can. My Grandma (Bubbe), the true rock of Gibraltar. Robert Smykowski for his technical contributions, legal prowess and friendship. My staff, for their continued patience with me and their ability to always make the impossible possible. And of course, all of you, my readers, and readers of my newsletter, *Mature American*, for asking the questions and thirsting for more knowledge.

Contents

Chapter 1

Introduction to protecting your hard-earned savings

Need and concern

You have home insurance if your house burns down and you save for retirement. But do you know how to protect against the loss of income caused by a disability or an illness that forces you into a long-term care facility? Whether you're already retired and are trying not to spend your last dollar before you die, or you're already caring for someone—perhaps your mother or father—*it's absolutely necessary that you understand how to protect your savings against a disability or long-term illness.* If you don't protect your savings, you won't be financially independent and you'll probably die broke! Don't let this happen to you. Our lawmakers have made it extremely difficult for you to understand the system. However, by reviewing resources such as this book and planning properly ahead of time, you can go far in protecting your assets from unexpected problems. Don't delay—start reading!

Don't fool yourself—it can happen to you

Disabled people are the largest minority in the United States, representing between 10 and 15 percent of the population. Rather than focusing on the financial difficulties that result from a loved one's death, you should consider what would happen if you or a loved one were alive and disabled. There may be as many as 200 car accidents per hour. That sounds like a staggering number, but there are almost *1,200 new disabilities per hour*, according to the National Safety Council. What does this mean to you? Depending on your age and other factors, such as your occupation, general health, sex and family history, you have more than a 50 percent chance of suffering a disability that will last more than 90 days.

Catastrophes within the next hour...

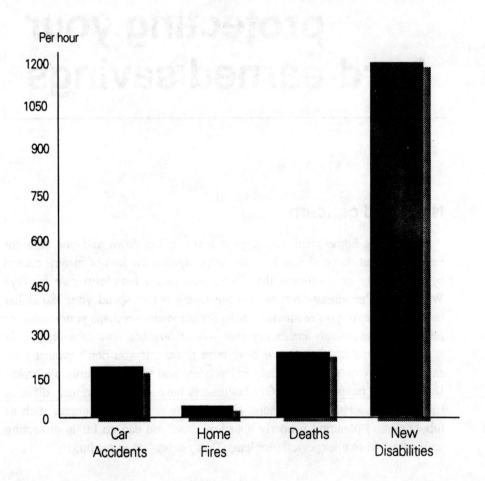

Source: National Safety Council

Consider the chances of at least one disability lasting 90 days or more before age 65.

Chance of Disability

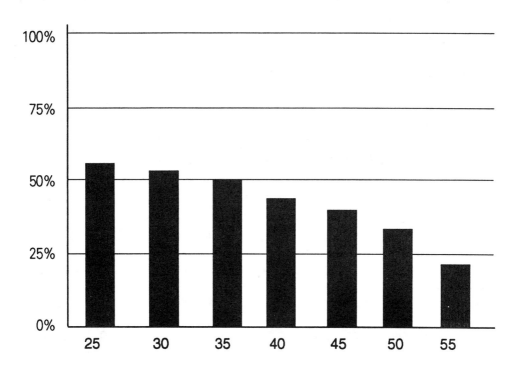

Source: 1985 Commissioners Individual Disability Table A

A disability is expensive

If you are part of a two-income family, the loss of one income can have a dramatic impact on your financial stability. Will one spouse's income be sufficient to support both of you, as well as add to your savings for retirement, vacations and everything else? Consider your earning potential. If you are 45 years old, make $50,000 per year and expect to work until you reach age 65, you would earn about $1,000,000. That is a great deal of money to make up. When someone becomes disabled, certain expenses go up, such as basic medical supplies, increased mileage or gasoline usage for trips to the doctor or hospital, etc. Statistics show that even if you save 10 percent of your income, a disability can wipe out *10 years of savings in just one year!* Disabilities are a real possibility and they are unbelievably expensive.

Based on your current income, these are your potential earnings to age 65.

	Annual Income					
Age	$25,000	$50,000	$75,000	$100,000	$150,000	$200,000
30	875,000	1,750,000	2,625,000	3,500,000	5,250,000	7,000,000
35	750,000	1,500,000	2,250,000	3,000,000	4,500,000	6,000,000
40	625,000	1,250,000	1,875,000	2,500,000	3,750,000	5,000,000
45	500,000	1,000,000	1,500,000	2,000,000	3,000,000	4,000,000
50	375,000	750,000	1,125,000	1,500,000	2,250,000	3,000,000
55	250,000	500,000	750,000	1,000,000	1,500,000	2,000,000
60	125,000	250,000	375,000	500,000	750,000	1,000,000

What is the likelihood that I will need some type of long-term care?

Before answering this question, you need to know exactly what constitutes *long-term care*. Long-term care is usually equated to a nursing home. However, this is not the whole picture. Long-term care could include a *nursing home, home health care, adult day care, respite care, custodial or intermediate care* and a myriad of in-betweens.

The good news is that we are living longer. Unfortunately, that does not always mean we are healthier. While our lives may be prolonged, we have a greater chance of suffering a disability. Chronic disabilities ranging from arthritis to diabetes dramatically increase with age. Here are some discouraging statistics:

- The elderly population in this country (those aged 65 and older) increased from 26 million in 1980 to 33 million in 1990. By the year 2020, this number is expected to exceed 52 million, which represents a 63 percent increase over the current elderly population. This number will equal about 20 percent of the total United States population.

- Forty-three percent of those age 65 and over will enter a nursing home at some time in their lives.

- Fifty percent of all couples are impoverished within six months of one spouse's admission into a nursing home.

- The average stay in a nursing home is more than 2.7 years. For victims of such debilitating diseases as Alzheimer's, the average stay can run as long as five to 10 years (according to the 1991 edition of "Aging American, Trends and Projections," prepared by the U.S. Senate Special Committee on Aging).

Long-term care costs can be overwhelming

Why is it possible to go broke after you retire? A key reason will be not having saved for long-term care costs. The average annual cost of long-term care can range from $36,000 to $60,000. That doesn't even include all the extra expenses and incidentals, such as grooming, gifts and medical supplies that the sick patient will need. The healthy spouse has living expenses, as well. The overall costs are astronomical.

Don't I already have disability coverage?

You may think that if you become disabled, you are covered by your employer's policy or by Social Security. You will learn more about this coverage later in the book. However, the simple fact is that most employer-sponsored plans cover only a short-term disability and usually pay a maximum of 60 percent of your salary. Could you live on 60 percent of your salary?

Furthermore, don't assume that Social Security will cover disability. Most people who are disabled simply can't work or cannot work in the same capacity as they did before they became disabled. Social Security's definition of disability is quite strict and limited. A huge percentage of people are disabled but do not qualify for the Social Security disability benefits.

Won't Medicare cover a long-term stay?

This is such a wild misconception! The requirements for Medicare are quite stringent and even if you do qualify for it, the coverage is only for short-term duration. In fact, *Medicare pays only about 2 percent of all long-term nursing stays.*

Likewise, if you think your Medicare supplement (Medi-Gap) policy or HMO will cover you, think again. If you're fortunate enough to have any supplemental coverage, it is probably only for a certain type of care facility that meets specific criteria for a maximum of 100 days.

I won't go into a convalescent care facility and I won't let my family members go into one, either

Let me share with you a true experience. My maternal grandmother recently had a stroke. After getting over the initial shock and then the euphoria that she would survive, realization set in. Once her vital signs stabilized, the doctors planned to release her from the hospital. However, she lost all feeling on one side of her body. She couldn't walk, drive or do much else. She needed 24-hour care. All of her children work, and as much as everyone wanted to help, we were stuck. Even if my mother were able to quit her job to care for her, she would not have been able to lift her.

There have been some poignant articles about children trying to act as caregivers for their parents. To care for their parents, some children use vacation time, bring their folks to live with them, quit their jobs, etc. Unfortunately, most of these arrangements don't work. Assuming you could afford it and don't mind the adjustments you must make to your own lifestyle, you must be a full-time nurse. You're likely to go insane just trying to keep up with all your responsibilities.

Many husbands assume they will take care of their wives. Guess what? Chances are, the men will be in a care facility themselves or in another world (the Great Beyond) by the time a crisis comes up.

Still others say, "I simply will not let it happen to me." I wish we all had that much control. However, strokes and other illnesses occur very suddenly. Many Alzheimer's victims do not even realize there is a problem. You have no advance warning when you're in a car accident. You may have to enter a care facility whether you want to or not. The fastest growing age group in the U.S. includes those who are 85 years and older. Unfortunately, the majority of people in that age group will need to spend time in a care facility.

Summary

It's not pleasant to think that you or a loved one will end up needing some type of long-term care. After all, you're healthy and you take care of yourself, so there's no reason to expect that you will have to go into a nursing home or require other long-term care. Unfortunately, the statistics prove this reasoning wrong. Nearly half of everyone over age 65 will need some type of long-term care, and some 50 percent of the people who enter nursing homes will deplete all their savings within six months!

While you can't change this discouraging picture, you can prepare yourself. You and your family must prepare yourself financially for the time when you or a spouse needs long-term care. The time for this work is well *before* you need the care, not when you're ill or disabled.

Reading this book is an excellent start. This chapter tells you why you have to plan for long-term care. The following chapters will describe in detail the various strategies for protecting your assets, what insurance policies are available and how to find the long-term care facility that best meets your needs.

Chapter 2

Disability overview

As discussed earlier, the probability that you will become disabled in some form or another is very high—higher than the likelihood of a fire in your home, an unexpected illness, a car accident, etc. What would you do if you had an accident or a stroke, or got cancer? Whether the sickness is temporary or permanent, could you afford the lost income and the higher expenses caused by the disability? You need to understand what to do if something does happen.

I call this my "three-legged" stool. If you become disabled, you have three main sources of assistance:

- Employer-sponsored disability plans.
- Social Security disability benefits.
- Private disability insurance.

Employer-sponsored disability plans

The good news is that about half of all employers with 100 or more employees have some type of disability coverage. The bad news is that half don't, and even the half that does often has only mediocre coverage

Typical disability plans include coverage up to 60 percent of your salary (with a maximum, usually between $4,000 and $5,000 per month) while you're disabled. The coverage generally stops after a relatively short period of time. Few plans offer coverage that lasts until age 65, when it is assumed that you will be eligible for Social Security. In addition, many of these plans will not start paying benefits until either 90 days or six months after the onset of your disability.

Another problem is the restrictive clauses that are often found in the plans. For example, your employer's policy will pay a long-term disability benefit for two years. However, the policy will only pay if you cannot work in any capacity. Let's assume you used to be a secretary for a company and acquired carpal-tunnel syndrome. If the company offers you a position as a messenger or a spokesperson—some spot that is presumably not affected by your disability—you must take the job or you will not receive the disability payments.

The coverage can be voluntary or mandatory. If coverage is mandatory, find out everything you can about it so you will be aware of what the policy covers. Understanding your employer's coverage will help you decide whether you need to get your own disability insurance to fill the gaps in your employer's policy.

If the coverage is optional, it is still usually a good idea to sign up, depending on the costs. A group policy is usually fairly cost-effective even if it does not cover everything that needs to be covered. However, you should first compare the costs of the group plan to the costs of a private policy. Also, if you and your spouse both work, see whether you qualify for discounts by taking coverage for both of you.

Americans with Disabilities Act

In 1992, the Americans with Disabilities Act of 1990 (ADA) became effective. This Act applies to all employers with 25 or more employees for the first two years; thereafter, employers with 15 or more employees will be covered.

The ADA definition of a person with disabilities is different than Social Security's definition. For purposes of the ADA, the disabled person is defined as: any person with a physical or mental impairment that substantially limits one or more of the major life activities of an individual.

The purpose of the Act is to require every employer to reasonably accommodate a disability of an applicant or employee, unless it would be a financial hardship to the employer. The accommodations are broad and could include such things as:

- Modifying equipment or work schedules.

- Providing alternate forms of training materials.

- Reassigning a person to another vacant position.

The ADA further prohibits employers from other practices that might result in discrimination because of a disability such as conducting a physical exam prior to hiring an employee.

	QUESTIONS TO ASK YOUR EMPLOYER ABOUT YOUR DISABILITY POLICY
1	Is the coverage optional or mandatory? Further, how long do you have to be with the company before you are covered under the plan?
2	What percentage of your salary is covered? Is there a "cap" on benefits? (For example, the policy will pay you 60% of your benefits up to a maximum of $3,000 per month regardless of your salary.)
3	Before your disability benefits begin, is it mandatory that you use your sick and vacation days?
4	What is the policy's definition of a disability? Meaning, does it have to be a total disability? If they can find you another job within the company, do you have to take it? For example, if you are a typist and acquire carpal tunnel syndrome and can no longer perform the tasks that you were hired for, do they consider you disabled, or if they find you another job not requiring manual labor, is that okay? What if your disability is partial, and you can work part-time? Will they pay you for the loss in wages? Some diseases are progressive (i.e., multiple sclerosis). Will you receive partial disability pay as your work hours are reduced? AIDS is a big problem today. Will your plan cover you, and at what point, when you are diagnosed with HIV or AIDS? Other plans define disability using the Social Security definition. This is a very stringent definition (see applicable section in this book). If you don't qualify under this definition, although you might still be disabled, will you get any benefits? Still other plans distinguish between physical and mental disabilities. If you have a mental impairment, will you be covered?
5	Does the plan have a preexisting condition clause? Meaning, if you went to the doctor several times for lower back pain prior to your employment and then filed for disability after gaining employment, would you receive it?
6	What is the elimination period? Meaning, what is the waiting period after the onset of disability before you can begin collecting disability benefits?
7	How long will benefits last? Can they stop in two years, three years, or go on indefinitely?
8	Will benefits stop (or be reduced) should Social Security begin to pay?

Again, the ADA is modified on a state-by-state basis and there are many strict regulations. If you need specific information, you should talk to your state or county labor department which monitors compliance with the ADA.

Disabilities are real and should not be taken lightly. You should understand your employer-sponsored plan and how you can protect yourself.

Why employers must know about the Americans with Disabilities Act

If you are an employer you can get into serious trouble if you don't comply with the ADA. Many employers are being sued as a result of improper treatment of employees, ex-employees, or would-be employees.

TIPS FOR EMPLOYERS TO AVOID PROBLEMS RESULTING FROM THE AMERICANS WITH DISABILITIES ACT

1	Make sure that you make reasonable accommodations for disabled employees. The purpose is to clear the way for a disabled employee to still carry out their job duties.
2	If you feel that an employee cannot carry out the job duties because of a disability, you must prove it. Understand this applies to potential employees, promotions of current employees, and firing of employees.
3	Even if you make reasonable accommodations for a disabled employee, and still feel they are no longer qualified, you have to prove they are not qualified.
4	Be careful of what people might consider a disability and try to prove in court. It could range from: carpal tunnel syndrome, to someone in a wheelchair, to obesity, to a badly burned individual.
5	Many experts feel that the best defense from a disability lawsuit is a detailed job description. These documents should be carefully prepared, implemented, and reviewed regularly by competent personnel. In each description, state all job duties, and the importance of each one. List what is required, including: appearance, physical needs, and mental needs. Think of the logic: If you don't have a solid job description, how can an employer argue against a claim from an employee that he or she can do their job?

Summary

There are three primary sources of disability coverage—private policies, employer coverage and government assistance. If employed, you should immediately review your company's disability policy. Find out what disability benefits you would receive, for what length of time and under what circumstances. This information is as important as your salary. The chances that you will have to use the disability coverage are far greater than you think. Not paying attention to your disability policy before you need it could cost you a great deal of time, money and aggravation in the future.

If you are an employer, you have even more to worry about. You will need to provide ample disability coverage at a reasonable cost. Employers must evaluate different policies and read between the lines to evaluate the extent of the coverage. Don't rely on your insurance agent's verbal description of the policy. Make sure you read the entire policy and any documents related to the coverage. In addition, an employer must keep the Americans with Disabilities Act in mind when making any hiring, firing and promotion decisions. The ADA should not be ignored; penalties include monetary fines and the possible loss of government loans or other assistance.

Chapter 3

Social Security disability

You may now have your own disability coverage; perhaps you feel that you can't afford it or you assume that you'll qualify for disability coverage under Social Security. Unfortunately, that's a dangerous assumption. Although Social Security does pay disability benefits to some qualified individuals, it's far more difficult to qualify for this coverage than you realize.

You should first understand the government rules on Social Security disability and then how you will be able to apply for benefits.

This chart shows how much Social Security disability pays each month, the tax on employee and employer as well as how much of your income is subject to this tax.

SOCIAL SECURITY DISABILITY BENEFITS 1995 FIGURES	
Figures used to determine a worker's insured status are revised annually and are generally published in a November issue of the Federal Register. Figures raising presumptions about ability to work are revised periodically.	
Average monthly benefit for disabled worker	$661.00
Tax rate for employee and employer	7.65 percent each
Tax rate for self-employed	15.30 percent
Maximum annual income subject to social security tax	$61,200
Quarter of coverage	$630 equals one quarter of coverage

Determining Social Security disability benefits for eligible workers and their families

Legislation recognizes that eligible workers and their families should have coverage in case of a disability. The Social Security disability program is a good start and provides some help. But, you should not assume it will cover all your disability needs.

The problem is that the Social Security Administration defines disability differently than you or I would. As a result, it is often difficult to receive Social Security disability benefits.

There are two separate types of disability programs—the Supplemental Security Income (SSI) and Social Security Disability Insurance. This chapter deals with the latter, Disability Insurance Benefits (DIB), also known as Title II Benefits of the Social Security Act. The purpose of this Act is to provide monthly benefits to workers and other eligible recipients who become disabled.

Requirements to receive disability insurance benefits

1. You must be disabled according to the Social Security definition. The definition states that a disability is an inability to engage in any substantial gainful activity by reason of any medically deter-minable physical or mental impairment which is expected to result in death or which has lasted or can last for a continuous period of not less than 12 months.
2. For a person to receive disability insurance, that person must be fully insured.

There is a difference between being fully insured for retirement benefits and fully insured for disability benefits. To be fully insured for disability purposes, you need to have worked at least five of the 10 years prior to becoming disabled. In Social Security jargon, you must have worked at least 20 quarters in the 40-quarter period ending in or after the quarter when you became disabled.

Assume you worked regularly from 1960 until 1990, and then stopped working because of a disability. You would have disability insured status for 10 years after 1990 (40 quarters or 10 years).

Born After 1929 Become Disabled At Age:	Credits You Need:
31 through 42	20
44	22
46	24
48	26
50	28
52	30
54	32
56	34
58	36
60	38
62 or older	40

If you become disabled before your 31st birthday, the rule is modified to one-half of the quarters between the quarter after the one in which you reached age 21 and the quarter of the onset of the disability. However, the minimum is six quarters of coverage.

1. For Disability Insurance Benefits (DIB) there is a five-month waiting period from the date you apply before you will receive benefits.

2. Families and dependents may also receive benefits (See section on disability benefits for worker's family, divorcees, children and survivors).

3. Certain disabilities that do not fall under the previous definition can be covered. One such disability is blindness.

4. These benefits are for everyone who is disabled, regardless of income or assets. You can even have a spouse actively working and still receive benefits. This is different than Supplemental Security Income (SSI) which is a program based on financial need.

Further definition of disability requirements

The Department of Health and Human Services has set up a rigorous evaluation system to determine if you are truly disabled. At any point, if the agency feels that you are not disabled, the evaluation is stopped and you are not granted DIB. The process is as follows:

1. You cannot perform any substantial or gainful work due to a medically determined physical or mental impairment that is expected to result in death or that has lasted, or can be expected to last continuously for at least 12 months.

   In some cases you are expected to try to obtain gainful employment. In other situations, you are allowed to try to work while still receiving disability insurance.

2. Your disability must be *severe*. This means you have to be significantly limited because of a physical or mental condition. There are lists of impairments that are used to determine a disability.

3. If you can't return to your previous job but you can still perform in a substantial and gainful capacity in another vocation, you may not qualify, or you may receive a trial disability period.

4. If you are age 55 or older, the disability rules state that you must be able to do comparable work to what you have previously done.

Special rules for blindness

It is the government's intent to make it easier for blind persons to receive DIB. The official definition of blindness means the better eye cannot be corrected to 20/200 vision or you have tunnel vision.

A blind person does not need to meet the 20-out-of-40-quarters test. However, to be covered, blind individuals must be fully insured.

Disability benefits for a worker's family, divorcees, children and survivors

Almost identical rules apply for family benefits as do benefits for families of insured Social Security workers. (For additional information on this topic, read my book *The Complete Guide to Social Security and Medicare*).

Rules are strict for divorcees. For the most part, should you remarry, you will lose the benefits.

For a fully insured worker's survivors, a family is entitled to disability benefits. This is true even if the deceased worker was not entitled to disability benefits. Furthermore, if a surviving family member is disabled, the individual may be paid disability benefits earlier or longer than he or she would normally receive regular survivors' benefits. To be eligible as a disabled family member (widow, divorced spouse, etc.), the individual must meet the same disability test applied to workers age 50 or older.

Disabled widow or widower

If the widow or widower is age 50 or older, and was married to someone who received disability or was fully insured, he or she is eligible for benefits. If the widow or widower remarries before age 50 or before the onset of disability, he or she will not be entitled to disability widow benefits.

The survivor must have been married to the deceased person for at least nine months prior to the worker's death, or be the mother or father of the worker's child.

Child benefits

If a child is a dependent of a deceased worker, the child may be eligible for benefits even if the worker was not eligible for them at the time of death. The worker needs to have been fully insured, or covered by Social Security for at least six of the 13 quarters immediately preceding disability or death.

The child must be:

1. Under age 18; or

2. A full time student under age 19; or

3. Disabled and have been disabled prior to his or her 22nd birthday.

How much payment is provided with disability benefits?

Obviously this answer varies, depending on your circumstances. Generally, to determine your benefits, you would figure what the disabled person's Primary Insurance Amount (PIA) would be at normal retirement age. However, the formula used to determine your Primary Insurance Amount, and Average Indexed Monthly Earnings (AIME) is different for calculating a disabled benefit and retired benefit.

Furthermore, a disability benefit will end when:

1. You reach retirement age and receive normal Social Security benefits.

2. Your disability ends.

3. You pass on.

How to file a claim for disability coverage

1. You must complete a Disability Benefits Application Form (SSA-16) at the onset of your disability. This form must be filed at a district or branch office. Look in your yellow pages under United States Government Services for the location of the office nearest you.

2. There is a five-month waiting period from the onset of the disability before DIB will be paid.

3. The local or district SSA office will determine if you are fully or currently insured for disability status.

   If you are deemed ineligible based on insured status (this is before they even get to your disability), you have 60 days to request a review of this determination and submit additional evidence.

   If you pass the insured status, your file will be forwarded to the state agency, known as the State Disability Determination Service, which is responsible for determining whether you are disabled.

4. The State Disability Determination Service will request and verify medical records and will probably have you examined by an approved medical professional.

   During this process, it is critical that you do everything you can to expedite your application. Make sure your doctors are sending the medical records that are requested. There are many ways you can prove disability. Send all supporting evidence with your original application. This material can include:

   - Documents from other agencies who have found you are disabled or eligible for workers' compensation.

   - Letters from previous employers or co-workers.

   - Statements from relatives or other people you live with about how the disability has impaired or affected your life.

5. Once all the information is obtained, the State Disability Determination Service will notify the Office of Disability Operations of its decision. This office administers the disability programs for the SSA. It reviews the state agencies determination, conducts ongoing investigations and reviews, etc.

The Social Security Administration must review at least 65 percent of all the state agency determinations. The SSA has the discretion to deny coverage should it feel justified in doing so.

What to do if you are denied disability insurance

Appeal the decision! You have 60 days from your receipt of the notice of denial to ask for reconsideration.

If your reconsideration appeal is again denied, you should request a hearing. To request a hearing, you must file form HA-501 with your district office. You should receive a hearing date within three to six months after filing. Usually, you are given notice 20 days prior to the hearing.

Unfortunately, the hearing takes you back to the point of starting the application process all over. Not only must you prove that you are disabled, but you have to prove you are insured for disability benefits. (In fact, you should review your Social Security file prior to the hearing). You can contact the local Office of Hearing and Appeals (OHA) or the national office 5107 Leesburg Pike, Falls Church, VA 22046; 703-235-3800. You will hear the results of the hearing roughly three to 10 weeks after the proceedings.

The appeals process summarized:

1. Request reconsideration.
2. Hearing held by an administrative law judge.
3. Review by appeals court judge.
4. Federal court review.

After receiving disability benefits, you will continually be reviewed

It is important to understand that you will be continually reviewed after you begin receiving disability payments. (You will also be reviewed when you begin receiving SSI benefits.) The review process is designed to show that you are still disabled. All relevant information will be reviewed and studied.

Usually, "borderline" disability cases, where a recovery is expected, will receive a review within six to 18 months. If the disability is predicted to be permanent but a recovery is possible, your case will probably be reviewed every three years. If a recovery or improvement is not expected, your case will probably be reviewed every five to seven years by the Social Security Administration to see if you're still disabled and still eligible for payment.

Summary

By law, all employees and employers pay for Social Security disability coverage through taxes on salaries. However, even though you pay these taxes, you don't automatically qualify for coverage. You will have to apply for the coverage, providing medical information to the Social Security administration. If you do qualify for benefits, Social Security will monitor your condition to see whether benefits should be continued as you recover from your disability. If your application is denied, you should appeal and justify your application for disability. Even if you're presently healthy, you should still understand how Social Security disability coverage works. If you comprehend the system now, when you don't need it, you'll have an easier time applying for disability coverage if and when you do need it.

Chapter 4

Supplemental Security Insurance (SSI)

Definition and eligibility

If you consider all of the Social Security programs and entitlement programs (since you paid into the system, you are entitled some benefit), the Supplemental Security Income (SSI) program is most similar to a welfare-type program. Eligibility requirements as well as the benefits are quite different from the programs discussed thus far.

The SSI program is administered by the Social Security Administration (SSA) and therefore is federally financed. SSI is meant to insure that there is a national minimum level of income for certain citizens. The program is designed to provide a monthly cash benefit to various qualified individuals, usually disabled, low-income or blind individuals. Roughly 4.5 million people are currently receiving SSI benefits in the United States.

MAXIMUM FAMILY BENEFITS FOR 1995

MONTHLY MAXIMUM	INDIVIDUAL	COUPLE
Basic Federal Payment:	$458	$687

Income Limits:
   With Earned Income:
   With Unearned Income:
	$1,001
	478
		$1,459
		707

Asset Limits (Annual):	$2,000	$3,000

Safeguard Your Hard-Earned Savings

While SSI has some similarities to the Social Security Disability Insurance Program, there are many significant differences. There are four broad requirements for eligibility. The following chart is a summary:

MAIN REQUIREMENTS FOR SSI ELIGIBILITY

1	AGE	You must be (A) 65 years of age or older, or (B) blind, or (C) disabled. The definition of an adult who is disabled is very similar to Disability Definition for Social Security Disability Insurance benefits (see explanation). To determine if a child (under age 18) is eligible is defined as, "any medically determinable physical or mental impairment of comparable severity (to that of an adult)". Basically, they are looking to see if you can function independently, appropriately, and effectively in an age-appropriate manner.
2	MEDICAL CONDITION	You may qualify if you are blind (defined the same for SS Disability Insurance).
3	CITIZENSHIP AND RESIDENCY REQUIREMENTS	You must be living in the United States (including Washington D.C., Northern Mariana Islands, but not Puerto Rico). You must also be a citizen of the United States, or an alien lawfully admitted for permanent residence or permanently residing in the United States (under that legal definition).
4	INCOME AND ASSET TEST	This is a discussion in and of itself. Basically, you have countable income (and income not counted), as well as countable assets. In 1994, singles are allowed countable earned income up to $977, or $466 of unearned income, per month. A couple living alone, in a private household is allowed to earn (of earned income) $1,423, or $689 of unearned income. In terms of assets (or they like to use the word "resources") you are allowed for individuals, $2,000 or less; for married, $3,000 or less.

SSI has strict definitions of what is considered countable income and what is not.

Countable income

1. All sources of money received. This includes income in any currency, checks or anything else representing income, such as gold. If you are given things in lieu of money as compensation, such as clothing and shelter, these things are part of your income.

2. All earned income. This includes income you get from a work program at some type of care facility.

3. All unearned income. This includes, but is not limited to Veterans Benefits, Workers Compensation, alimony, pensions, gifts, interest, annuities, dividends, rents, royalties, etc.

Noncountable income

1. The first $20 per month you receive from any source except public assistance.

2. The first $65 per month of earned income.

3. One-half of all your earned income over $65 month.

4. Irregular income (such as a gift or occasional dividend) up to $20 per month.

5. Housing assistance from a federal housing program.

6. Food stamps.

7. Work-related expenses for blind or disabled persons which are paid through public assistance.

8. Amounts from tuition and fees paid from grants and fellowships.

9. Impairment-related work expenses.

Countable assets

1. Any type of real estate and additions, such as swimming pools, excluding personal residences.

2. Personal property including home furnishings, jewelry, etc.

3. Anything broadly defined as an investment. This includes bank accounts, checking accounts, etc.

Noncountable assets

1. Your personal residence as long as you are living there.

2. Personal property valued up to $2,000.

3. One car.

4. The cash value of life insurance worth $1,500 or less.

5. Income-producing property regardless of its value as long as it is used for a trade or business and is essential to your support. For example, if you're a carpenter, your tools are noncountable assets. This may not seem logical: If you have income-producing property, then you are probably producing income. If the income total is too high, you would be ineligible for SSI.

6. Any property, items or resources needed and approved as self-support mechanisms for your disability.

7. Up to $6,000 of the equity value of nonbusiness property used to produce goods or services essential to daily activities. This is known as the $6,000/6 percent rule. The property must have a net annual return equal to at least 6 percent of the excluded equity value of the property. If the return is less than 6 percent, then this exclusion only applies if the lower return is caused by circumstances beyond your control (if, for example, you get sick) and you expect that the property will again produce a 6 percent return.

These income and asset tests for SSI are very similar to those of other programs such as Medicaid. Similar methodology is used for various entitlement programs and the tests are designed to limit eligibility to people who are essentially poverty stricken. To minimize the impact of these tests, you can plan ahead to legally shift your balance sheet so that you can shelter certain assets.

Gifting or leaving money to a child who is receiving SSI

As you might expect, a major concern for some parents is how to use estate planning and trusts to make sure a disabled child who receives SSI assistance is protected and can receive an inheritance without being deemed ineligible for SSI. This is something you will need to discuss with an attorney or financial advisor who is familiar with SSI regulations.

It is probably easier to gift someone assets instead of income. The income rules are strict while the asset rules allow for greater interpretation. The following ideas are based on strategies used by some elder-care experts. However, as with all specific questions for any subject in this book, you should consult an attorney who specializes in estate planning, elder-care law and/or disability law. The rules vary by state and even by county. Also, precedent is set every day in the courts. You should view this section as an introduction to some possible strategies for leaving property to a child who receives SSI.

Establishing trusts has been the predominant method of giving children assets without having the children lose the SSI benefits. With a trust, the recipient cannot have the assets, does not receive the income and does not have access to the funds and therefore, it is not part of the countable assets. If the SSI beneficiary does receive any of the income from a trust, the income would be included in the countable income at that time.

Keep in mind, however, there is also case law that shows many failed attempts at using trusts. If an advisor recommends that you set up a trust, ask the advisor why the trust will work. Ask for supporting case studies. This situation is too important to trust (no pun intended) anyone blindly.

Irrevocability of the trusts seems to be the key to the successful use of trusts for SSI recipients. A Medicaid Qualifying Trust is one popular type of trust that actually works to *disqualify* you for Medicaid (for further explanation see the Medicaid section of this text), but may be more useful for SSI benefits. Special Needs Trusts, Offshore Trusts, Craven Trusts and Disability Trusts are also types of trusts that people have used in an effort to protect SSI benefits for individuals who might have received or may still be receiving money.

Some of the best ways I have seen trusts created are in conjunction with judicial proceedings. For example, you could go to court to prove the individual is incompetent and needs a guardian or conservator. Such a trust is not voluntary and therefore would seem to comply with SSI regulations.

Remember, too, that a trust that works to protect SSI benefits may not work for Medicaid purposes. This is critical since SSI usually goes hand in hand with Medicaid benefits. You don't want to qualify for one and disqualify yourself for the other. Creating the right trust for SSI could disqualify you for Medicaid.

Medicaid and SSI have similar asset and income limitations. But, SSI does not have stringent rules governing how you give away money prior to going on SSI. Medicaid has very stringent rules known as look-back or 36-month rules. SSI recipients can transfer money at any time, without restriction, prior to applying for SSI benefits. However, if you give away money under SSI rules, you may disqualify yourself from Medicaid benefits.

Make sure any advice you receive takes into consideration rules for both SSI and Medicaid.

Although fancy estate planning along with the creative use of trusts might enable you to "work" within the requirements of the programs, it often makes sense not to bother with elaborate estate plans. Assume you have two children, one who is disabled and one who is not disabled. If you believe your well child is responsible, why not give all your money to that child, and have a verbal agreement that he or she is responsible for the disabled child? This arrangement would seem to be a sound one except that if the well child is sued, divorced or goes bankrupt, he or she might take all the money and not leave any funds for the disabled child. Therefore, the best solution for this situation is to use an irrevocable trust arrangement. You can include a lifetime benefit along with a spend-thrift provision that will prevent the well individual from depleting the estate because of mismanagement or credit problems.

Social Security Disability Insurance is not Supplemental Social Security Income (SSI)

Assets or other income is not a factor in determining your benefits under the Social Security disability (DIB) program. Your eligibility for DIB is based on your past work experience. For SSI, on the other hand, income and assets are factored into your eligibility and you don't need any work experience.

What are the benefits from SSI?

The basic Federal payment for a single person was $446 a month in 1994, or $669 for a couple. As with most Federal programs, these amounts are adjusted annually, according to the increases in the Consumer Price Index (CPI).

The amount of money you will receive varies, depending on three primary factors:

1. Other income of you and your spouse.
2. Whether you live with your children and do not contribute to household expenses.
3. Whether anyone else is providing you with any means of support.

Also, you should be aware that some states pay their own benefits so you may receive more benefits than you expect. Check with your local Social Security office to see if you qualify for this additional money.

Applying for SSI

If you think that you qualify for SSI, you can apply either at your local Social Security office or by mail. You will need your Social Security card and proof of identity and age (usually a birth certificate, driver's license or passport is sufficient). You will also need to provide income information including details of your mortgage, if you have one, and a list of your assets, such as bank accounts or stock holdings.

Since SSI is so important, I encourage you to get help in completing your application. There are services that will help you fill out your forms or help expedite your application for no charge (see resources at the end of the book).

As with other decisions involving Social Security or the Health Care Financing Administration (HCFA), you have the right to appeal a decision if you're denied coverage. You should request an appeal form from your local Social Security office. Get help with the appeal form and good luck!

Summary

Supplemental Social Security income is an entitlement program designed to offer monthly benefits to citizens in need. Generally, you must be age 65 or older, have certain disabilities and have income and assets that fall below the set maximum limits. While you may have a certain disability and have little current income, you may have too many assets to qualify for this program. In order to reduce your assets, you may have to use various strategies to legally shelter your assets.

If you're in need, you should definitely apply for SSI coverage. Be fore-warned, however, that the rules of the program are as complicated as the tax code. Even if you are rightfully entitled to receive this assistance, getting through the system can be aggravating and difficult. You should research the rules yourself and get help so you can take advantage of the loopholes in the system.

Chapter 5

Private disability insurance

You probably don't want to hear that you will have to pay for more coverage or another expense, especially if it relates to insurance. However, the peace of mind and relief from stress this coverage offers you could be worth the expense. In fact, the coverage may not be as expensive as you think. But if it is so expensive that getting a disability policy would be a burden, then you may be able to qualify for benefits under one of the entitlement programs such as Supplemental Security Income, Food Stamps, Aid to Families with Dependent Children, etc. Remember, if you have assets or future income to protect, disability insurance is coverage that you can't afford to overlook.

First, review your employer's coverage to see what the policy covers. If your employer's policy is not sufficient, then you need to look into getting your own policy.

Private disability insurance is designed to pay you a monthly benefit if you become disabled. You should shop for a private disability policy as carefully as you would look for a new car. Research thoroughly all policies that you're considering.

How to evaluate a disability policy

1. *What is the insurance company's definition of disability?*

    This is probably the most important question you need to ask about disability coverage. Find out the specifics of the company's definition. Is it the same as Social Security's definition? Ideally, you should try to find a policy that is less restrictive than the Social Security definition of disability.

Some policies define a disability as simply "the inability to perform your job duties." Under this definition, if you cannot do your normal job duties, you are disabled. Sometimes, the definition spells out "your own occupation." In this case, even if you can do the duties of another job, if you can't do what you had been doing prior to the disability, then the insurer considers you disabled. Some policies say that you must be capable of "no gainful employment." This is almost as strict as Social Security's definition.

You should also see whether the policy has stipulations for the type of ailment that qualifies as a disability. For example, does a mental illness qualify you for disability?

2. *What is the premium cost and will the premium increase?*

One percent of your yearly income is the average premium for coverage equal to 70 percent of your income. Make sure you have a "non-cancellable" policy. The premiums don't change.

Premiums need to be carefully reviewed. Once you find out the initial cost of the premium, ask your agent whether it will go up as you get older or if you suffer several disabilities. Incidentally, some policies have inflation riders as well. If your disability does not occur for 10 more years, this type of coverage would pay more, based on the inflation rate or a fixed percentage over that period of time. For example, if your policy has a 5 percent annual inflation rider, your benefits would increase 5 percent per year.

3. *Is the policy renewable?*

Ask whether it is guaranteed renewable so that, regardless of what may happen in the future, as long as you pay your premium, the policy can never be canceled.

4. *How is the underwriting done on the policy?*

Here's one scenario: You have applied and are accepted for a policy. In the application, you were asked if you ever had lower back problems and you answered "no." One year after getting the policy you become disabled. The company denies your claim because they have now found out that five years ago you went to a doctor because of lower back pains. This isn't that uncommon.

Look for companies that do the underwriting when you apply for the policy. When you give the insurance company the completed application they have to do all the checking and underwriting they are going to do before accepting you. Once you are accepted they can not go back and amend the acceptance.

Other companies have what's commonly called a "two-year window," which means that after you own a policy for two years, the company cannot disqualify you for any reason. Let's assume that on the application for disability insurance you are asked if you hang-glide. You say no because you don't think you will anymore. However, after you get the disability policy you begin hang-gliding again without notifying the company. After two years, the company cannot disqualify you for this "false information" on your application. However, if you would have become disabled prior to the two-year window, you might not receive the disability benefit.

5. *When do benefits start and how long will they last?*

Do benefits start the day you become disabled—or six months later? This is an important consideration because you can reduce your premiums if you can save a three or six-month cash reserve on your own, and take a policy that does not begin to pay benefits for three or six months. You would lower your premium cost by 15 to 25 percent, depending on the policy. Perhaps, your employer-sponsored plan will pay for two years worth of coverage so you can take a policy that starts after your employer's policy stops covering you.

The length of the benefit varies as well. Many advocates (or agents in disguise) advise you to sign up for a policy that will pay until your death. However, if you are entitled to Social Security you will receive that benefit at age 65, so you shouldn't have a lifetime disability policy.

6. *What are the rules for pre-existing conditions?*

Assume that you have a lower-back problem. Will the company insure you for all disabilities except those related to your lower back? Sometimes a company says that if you are healthy for a certain time period, usually two years, it will then pay for a disability, even if it is related to your lower back.

7. *How much is the benefit and how is it calculated?*

This is a very tricky question. Let's take the earlier example where you had carpal-tunnel syndrome and could not be a typist any longer. You earned $30,000 per year. Now that you are un-employed, you use dictation to write a novel. The novel is a best seller and you make a million bucks. Will you still receive the disability benefits? Possibly. It depends on your policy.

Some policies state that they will only pay an amount equal to your loss of wages or "gross income." If you go out and earn more money than you were earning before the disability, you would not receive any benefits.

Other policies state that if you cannot do what you were doing at the time of disability, even if you enter another profession, it will pay the stated disability benefit of the policy.

The differences in policies affect the cost of the disability premium. You must also decide how much in benefits you want. Do you want a policy that pays 60 percent of your salary, 8 percent of your wages, etc.? You should first figure out how much you can afford to do without, and then weigh the premium costs of the policy to reach a compromise.

8. *Are the benefits taxable?*

The general rule is, if you take a tax deduction for the premium cost, then the benefit is taxable. However, if you do not take a tax deduction for the premium, the benefits are usually tax-free.

Hopefully you are not planning to use the insurance. So, if you need additional deductions for your tax return, then you should deduct the cost of the premium.

9. *What is the insurance company's rating?*

You need to know if the company is going to be in business far into the future. It would be a shame if you paid your premiums for many years and then found out the company went out of business leaving you with nothing. You would have no insurance and you would have wasted all the money you spent on the premiums. Look for companies that have been in business for preferably at least 10 years. Companies that have been writing policies for at least this long will have had to pay some benefits. Newer companies may have issued policies but could be undercapitalized and may not be able to make payments on all their policies. Companies should also have ratings of at least A or A+. The three big rating agencies include A.M. Best, Standard and Poor's and Moody's. The highest rating Best gives is A+ Superior. Standard and Poor's and Moody's give a highest rating of AAA.

10. *Is there a premium waiver?*

Most policies have a premium waiver. The waiver states that if you become disabled you no longer have to continue paying the premium.

11. *What about those fancy riders on the policy?*

Many agents will make claims about their policy while other try to fast talk you into a decision. Ask the agent to write down everything that he or she says about the policy.

Also, don't let anyone persuade you to take a policy you don't need. For example, some policies have a "compounding inflation rider," with the increase compounded onto a new amount each year. You should ask what the policy will cost you in five years.

Some polices have a "return of principal rider." This provision states that after you own a policy for a certain length of time, if you do not become disabled, some or all of your principal will be returned. However, the cost for this provision is often more expensive than its value. You probably could have taken the money it cost for this rider and invested and earned more than what you will get by receiving back your principal.

Special rules for the elderly

Many senior citizens are disabled. Some have chronic disabilities such as arthritis that affect their daily lives. It is important to note that many special services are available for disabled older Americans, such as disability programs, hotlines and other services.

If you're an older American on disability, you should contact an elder-care group to make sure that you get all the benefits you're entitled to.

Summary

There's no excuse for you not to plan what you would do if you became disabled. This is especially important if you're saving for your children's college costs or planning to retire soon. You must take the time to carefully evaluate private disability insurance. Because the policies are expensive and sometimes difficult to understand, you should do your research when you're healthy and don't have an immediate need for the policies. You have to be a savvy consumer: don't spend your hard-earned money on excessive coverage that isn't necessary; don't be tricked by eager insurance salespeople; look for ways to minimize your premiums and get everything the agent promises in writing. Also, make sure that you're maximizing your two primary sources of disability assistance—your employer's disability insurance and Social Security Disability.

Chapter 6

Long-term care and convalescent care overview

The first chapter of this book presented statistics showing the extraordinarily high percentage of people who are using or will need to use care facilities. This chapter will help you focus on what action you must take to address this problem today, before it is too late.

Acknowledging that long-term care is an issue you must deal with today is a good first step, but there are several significant decisions that you must make about long-term care. The most pressing concerns are the following:

- Determine the type of care you will need.

- Finding quality care.

- Assess the cost of the care.

- Protect yourself and your family against fraud.

This chapter will address these important issues. If you can determine the care you or a loved one needs, then find a quality provider of this care and do this without going broke or being defrauded, then you have accomplished your mission. This will be a very difficult assignment, so prepare yourself.

Determine the type of care you will need

Do you need skilled nursing care 24 hours a day? Do you want a place to live where you can get help preparing your meals and have access to nurses should you need them? Do you want to live in a lively active retirement community and, as your medical needs change, be able to take advantage of greater care that is available at the community? These are the questions that you should answer before you start to shop for a care facility.

Retirement communities have been developing at a rapid pace over the past decade. Both the number of communities as well as the types of communities have been increasing. This rapid growth can be attributed to three major factors—the baby boomers approaching their retirement age; the greater longevity of the population (In fact, the fastest growing segment of the population is the 85 and older category); and the inability of children to care for their aged parents because of the increase in two career families.

When people are asked in surveys what their concerns are for living arrangements as they get older, the most pressing concern is what will happen if their health fails. More than half of the people surveyed are interested in living in a place where meals, transportation, housekeeping and social activities are provided without limiting the residents' independence.

Many people want to move when they retire. There are many reasons for this inclination such as wanting a change of scenery; desiring to be closer to children and grandchildren; wanting a smaller home or one that is easier to manage; wanting to be near other retirees; needing easy access to activities or social structure and wanting the availability of good medical care if it is needed. The variety of retirement communities address these needs. Here's a brief look at the various types of retirement communities.

Independent living

Retirement communities seem to offer something for everyone. You can take advantage of activities, aerobic classes, golf, tennis, libraries, parties, etc. You know that you will have friends your age nearby. Still, it's important for you to evaluate a community carefully before you decide to move there. Living in a community is different that spending an afternoon with friends.

When evaluating a retirement community, answer the following questions:

1. *Will you enjoy it?*

     The amenities may sound appealing but will you take advantage of them? For example, some retirement communities charge for one prepared dinner every day. Will you enjoy eating dinner in the same location every night?

     To see whether you and a particular community seem like a good match, take a trial run. Vacation there for a week. Talk to several residents and ask them specific questions about their daily routines and their experiences in the community. Could you imagine yourself living in the community for an extended period of time?

2. *What is the cost?*

As in other stages of your life, you will generally have the option of renting or buying a home or apartment in a retirement community. The considerations are not so different than deciding to buy or rent outside a community. You must calculate the financial cost including a mortgage, possible appreciation of the property, the tax consequences of buying and your monthly outlay. In addition, you have to evaluate the non-financial factors such as whether you expect to stay in the community for an extended period of time or would have the option to walk away from your property if you suddenly decide to leave the area.

First, assume that you find a community that you must buy into. There are different arrangements within this type of community. Some communities have an entrance fee. If you're considering one of these communities, find out what the entrance fee includes, as well as whether you can sell your residence if you move, or get a refund if you leave or die.

Almost all communities have ongoing Homeowners Association (HOA) dues that can range from $200 to as high as $3,000 a month. You must also assume that these figures will increase over time, so when you review your budget to see whether you can afford the monthly fees, you must calculate a higher monthly fee, even if your monthly income is staying the same. To be safe, you should do several calculations, assuming the HOA increases will range from 5 to 10 percent.

3. *What are your plans if one spouse gets sick or dies?*

Hopefully, you and your spouse will be healthy and active when you start looking at retirement communities. But, it's essential that you assume that at some point in the future, one or both of you will get sick or require some type of medical care. Just as you're evaluating the amenities at the community, you have to look into the type of medical facilities available. Is there a hospital or care facility nearby? How expensive are these facilities? Assume that you will have ongoing expenses at the retirement community as well as the cost of care at a medical facility.

When you're looking at houses or apartments, you should also consider the possibility of having to care for a loved one at home. You may want to find a residence that has only one floor, few stairs or a bathroom and bedroom on the ground floor. Again, it's easier to plan now than to realize at some point in the future that your home will not easily accommodate a wheelchair or hospital bed.

As unpleasant a thought as it may be, you have to consider what you would do if your spouse dies. Would you want to stay in the community by yourself or would you want to move closer to other family members? Knowing that selling your house or share in the community will be easy can alleviate your concerns in this area.

Overall, retirement communities provide a terrific lifestyle for many people. They can be as comfortable as resorts, with activities and friends all in one location. However, you should be warned that many older people do get ripped off when they look for a retirement community. Sometimes, the buyers are so excited at the outward appearance of the community that they neglect to do their homework.

When evaluating a community, follow these steps:

- Visit several communities and talk to the residents. This will give you a handle on the community and can provide information to use when you're negotiating.

- Narrow your selection down to a few in the area and then begin negotiating.

- Tell the community representative that you are considering several communities in the area and are ready to start negotiating. Let the representative make an offer and then make a counteroffer. You may want to counteroffer for 10 to 15 percent less than the figure you're quoted by the community representative. Then, he or she may offer to throw in some extras for the quoted price, such as upgraded carpet, washer/dryer, etc. You will then have to figure out if this is really a good deal. Are you getting these amenities for less than what you would be pay if you had to buy them on your own? Finally, be fully prepared to walk away. Don't call back, and be firm. Wait for the community representative to call you back.

Continuing-Care Retirement Communities (CCRCs)

After independent living comes continuing-care communities (CCRCs). These two arrangements are similar except that the CCRC has additional medical staff and facilities available. The appeal of a CCRC is that you can maintain independent living but also have access to on-site care such as nursing should you need it. This convenience comes with a price, however. CCRCs tend to be very expensive options.

These types of communities usually offer apartment living arrangements with different levels of care, based on individuals needs. Usually, you start off living independently in your own apartment or a room in a shared apartment. Generally, you can have your own furniture and other personal items. The communities feature a wide array of services including beauty salons, free transportation, game rooms, libraries, pools and exercise facilities. In addition, these communities offer meal services, generally breakfast and/or dinner in the main dining room. Also, a medical professional such as a nurse is usually available at all times. Most rooms are equipped with help buttons for emergencies.

Many proponents of CCRC living say these communities are ideal for couples. If one spouse gets sick, the nursing care is available in the same community so the two of you won't be separated or have to go elsewhere for medical attention. You can also maintain your independence without having to worry about the upkeep of a house. The availability of nursing care and long-term care is certainly one of the primary advantages to CCRC. However, you should still evaluate a CCRC to see whether it meets your needs.

You should ask the following questions when you're comparing CCRCs:

1. Get a list of all the amenities. Ask whether free transportation is provided. Are classes held regularly? Is maid service available?

2. If you need to start using some of the medical services, how much will your fees increase? For example, if you require a nurse or aide to help you bathe, what additional fees will you have to pay?

3. If the CCRC is affiliated with a nursing home, are you guaranteed a bed? Or, will you have to put your name on a waiting list? Even if you're healthy now, you should still visit the nursing home. Inspect the home to see whether you would be comfortable there as well.

4. Find out who owns the care facility. Is it an independent operator or part of a large conglomerate? If the home is run by a smaller company, you should ask what happens if the company has financial difficulties. Obviously, you would not want to buy into a community with the expectation of using a care facility and then find out that it has shut down.

5. Find out all of the costs. If necessary, ask the community to break down the costs by month, year and type of service. By having a complete list of costs for all the communities you're considering, you can compare the costs for identical services.

POSSIBLE QUESTIONS TO ASK IN EVALUATING ASSISTED LIVING AND CCRC COMMUNITIES

1	First and foremost, does the home feel warm and desirable to live in?	Do you feel as though you could live there comfortably?
2	Is the location appropriate?	Is it close to shopping, hospitals, family, your doctor, etc.?
3	What impression does the staff give you?	This is critical - trust your gut reaction. Look for the subtleties: do they talk to residents like children? Do they know the residents' names? Are they genuinely helpful and cheerful?
4	Cleanliness	A clean home is essential. Observe how waste disposal is treated. What is the odor in the home?
5	Other residents	Are the other residents in the community the type of people you want to associate with? Can you make friends with them, are they hospitable?
6	Floor plan	Again, try it out. Do you have privacy? Are the cabinets easy to reach? Are there rails for walking assistance, etc.?
7	Miscellaneous	Try the food and look at a weekly menu. Make sure that you like the chef's cooking and choice of meals. Review the activity roster. Do they invite guests to speak, have book clubs, etc.?
8	Carefully review the quality of care you will receive there.	To accomplish this I would ask if there is a written plan for your care and what it is - i.e., therapy two days a week, walks, massage, etc. Are there different levels of care as your needs change? Does the care giver spend time with you individually assessing your needs? Does this facility have any connections with long-term care should you need it later? If so, is it Medi-Cal approved?
9	What are the costs?	This could be one of the most confusing questions you ask. First look for deals. See if there are any government or religious programs that offer assistance. Contact the Elder-Care Locator (1-800-677-1116). Contact the Area for the Aging. See if you qualify for any assistance. Ask what happens if you run out of money. Do they have a program for low-income clients? Are they affiliated with Medicaid in any way? Once you get the price list, start negotiating. Many of the incidentals (bathing, transportation, housekeeping, grooming) that may normally be extra charges can be received for no charge. Negotiate that they can't raise your rates for so many years. Show them that you are a good tenant and how it will make sense for them.
10	Insist on a contract prior to moving in, discussing all that you were told and promised.	My attitude is no contract, no deal. No way would I invest all that time and money without something in writing specifically reviewing all that you are anticipating. Make sure it is specified what the costs are. If additional services are needed, what are the additional costs? At what point can they rise, etc.? Again, in the costs, this is yours to bear. With that you will need to start considering how you will pay for this. Plus, if you will need to move to a nursing home/convalescent care facility, will you have enough money to pay these costs?

The largest initial expense is usually the equity buy-in. Depending on the community, this can range from $10,000 up through $100,000. Again, you should find out if this fee is refundable if you move, pass on or have to stay in the care facility for an extended period of time.

The second cost is the monthly rent. Find out how much the rent can increase and whether there is a maximum cap to the increases. Review all of the rate increases over the past 10 years, if the community has been open that long. See whether you can get a guarantee that your rate will not increase for a certain time period. Ask whether your rent will decrease if your spouse passes on.

The third type of fee arrangement is similar to a basic service plan with added charges should you require extra services. You pay a basic rate and know that medical attention is available if you need it. Then, when you use the medical services, you are charged additional fees. You should try to find out as much detail about the costs in these types of arrangements. Consider this arrangement very carefully since it's often difficult to find out exactly what the medical care will cost. You won't have peace of mind knowing there is available medical care nearby if you won't be able to pay for the care.

Assisted living

This is probably the most popular type of retirement community. Although CCRCs are a sound concept, many people don't move from their homes until they require assistance in day to day functions. Assisted care consists of a hybrid of housing, medical and general assistance amenities wrapped up into one package. Assisted living is really a combination of a CCRC and a nursing home that is relatively affordable.

People who need help in one or more daily living activities but don't need 24-hour-a-day care should consider assisted care. Daily living activities include bathing, eating, dressing, using the bathroom, etc. Assisted care facilities are often a good option if you find it difficult to care for a spouse or other loved one who needs help in these activities.

Assisted living residences and CCRCs don't have to meet the same standards as traditional long-term care nursing facilities. The latter facilities have to comply with different laws, licensing requirements and various Medicare and possibly Medicaid regulations. Because CCRCs and assisted living facilities don't have to comply with as many government regulations, their fees are usually lower. It's very important that you find out who licenses the facility and whether there is ongoing monitoring of the quality of care by a local government agency. Ask to see the license; don't rely on the word of an admissions officer.

When you're investigating a CCRC or assisted living residence, don't automatically give out your Medicare identification number. Some facilities have been known to bill Medicare for services that are not necessary or may not have even been performed.

You will have to carefully review the costs with your financial situation in mind. You know what you have in savings, income or investments that you will be able to use to pay for care, now and in the future.

Income tax considerations

When you're deciding where to live during retirement, tax considerations should be one of the factors you consider while making your decision. If you sell a home, you may incur capital gains tax or lose mortgage deductions, etc. The following is a list of the most important tax issues to evaluate:

- **Capital gains tax.** The Internal Revenue Code (Section 121) allows a homeowner who is age 55 or over to exclude the first $125,000 of capital gain on the sale of his or her principal residence. There are additional rules to this exclusion. You are only allowed to use this exclusion once. If you remarry later in life and your spouse has already used this exclusion, you cannot. In addition, you must have used the home as your principal residence for three out of five years (you could live in your home intermittently for this time period; it does not have to be a continuous period).

- **Medical expense deduction.** Many of you forget about the important Medical Expense Deduction (Section 213) that is available for housing arrangements such as nursing homes, where housing is incidental to the medically necessary health care. This medical expense deduction can help you save money in several ways. For example, if you are taking a mandatory IRA distribution, you will probably have a higher income tax and this deduction could help offset this amount.

   Under the current tax code, you need a certain amount of medical expenses in relation to your income before you qualify for a medical deduction. Sometimes, married couples don't qualify for this deduction. Some couples have gotten divorced or file separately. Before taking this step, you should talk to a tax expert.

- **Step-up in tax basis.** If you understand this little known concept, you could save yourself thousands of dollars. Assume a single person purchased a home years ago for $20,000 and the home is now worth $200,000. You gift the house or transfer the title to your children. Then you die and your children sell the property for $200,000.

What is their capital gain? The gain is based on your original basis of $200,000.

Now, if the children received the property as an inheritance at a fair market value of $200,000 and sold the house for $200,000, what is their capital gain? Chances are the tax is zero, as a result of the step-up in tax basis to the fair market value on the owner's death. This simply means the tax basis for the property is whatever the property was valued at as of the date of the owner's death or six months later. The same situation applies for married couples; however, half of the property may "step up" when the first spouse dies.

This could be a critical planning tool if you have highly appreciated property and are considering transferring the property. The step-up in basis applies to almost all appreciated property including real estate and securities such as stocks and bonds.

- **State taxes.** Many people retire to another state. This could be either advantageous or costly. Some states have property taxes while others don't. Some states have inheritance taxes. Some states don't tax pension or Social Security income.

  Before moving to another state, you should project out the numbers to see how the taxes impact your situation. Try to estimate the value of your estate on your death. Then you should project the inheritance tax. Compare these figures with a state that has no inheritance tax but has property taxes.

Summary

Undoubtedly, you and your spouse are looking ahead to an active and enjoyable retirement, but it's crucial that you accept the fact that it's quite likely that you or your spouse will require some type of medical care during your retirement. You should start planning for this care now, well before you need it. Don't wait until you need the care to begin doing the research.

Long-term care includes several levels of care along with different types of facilities. It's important that you visit several facilities to evaluate the medical care, amenities, cost and other "quality of life" factors. Usually, the first type of care you will consider is independent living. Here, you can have your own apartment, participate in many community activities and have access to medical care. The next type of care facility is a continuing care facility. Here, you can go from your own apartment into a room where additional medical care can be provided as well as other services to help you. Finally, if you need assistance with daily functions such as eating and bathing, you should look at an assisted care facility.

Chapter 7

Long-term care and convalescent care specifics

Introduction

In the United States there are more than 15,000 nursing homes with more than 1.8 million beds, and current occupancy rates are more than 90 percent. Twenty states have more than 75 percent of all the nursing home beds nationwide. These states include California, Texas, New York, Illinois, Ohio, Pennsylvania, Florida, Indiana, Missouri, Michigan, Wisconsin, Massachusetts, Minnesota, New Jersey, Louisiana, Georgia, Iowa, Tennessee, Oklahoma and Kansas.

Nursing homes can be nonprofit and profit. Generally, nursing homes are owned and operated by three main entities: large corporations, small privately owned mom-and-pop operations, and religious and church organizations.

This chapter will introduce you to the many types of long-term care that are available. You can choose a custodial care facility or home health care.

You should assume that some level of care is needed when a person is having difficulty performing daily routine tasks. These tasks are known as activities of daily living (ADL). You can usually divide the ADL into five main categories: eating or preparing a meal, walking, bathing, going to the toilet and dressing. ADL are sometimes divided even further to include maintaining one's finances, remembering basic responsibilities, etc.

In addition, as our life spans continue to increase, so do many chronic health problems and disabilities ranging from arthritis to heart disease.

Because of these health problems, you may also need some type of long-term care.

It's important to be aware that you can no longer view hospitalization as you did in the past. Hospitals used to be places that you stayed in until you got better. Today, however, because of the cost-containment measures of Medicare, the government will only pay for services that are medically necessary. Once a person's condition is stabilized, coverage will be discontinued. This does not mean a person will be better. For example, in the past, if you had a hip replacement, you probably stayed in the hospital for weeks. Now, in many cases, you are released from the hospital in a matter of days to recover with the aid of home health care or at some type of custodial care facility.

Home health care

One of the reasons home health care is increasing in popularity is because many seniors have difficulty performing only certain tasks. As you can see from the chart below, the activities most likely to cause trouble are bathing, walking and transferring. If a senior simply had help in the home, he or she might not need a care facility.

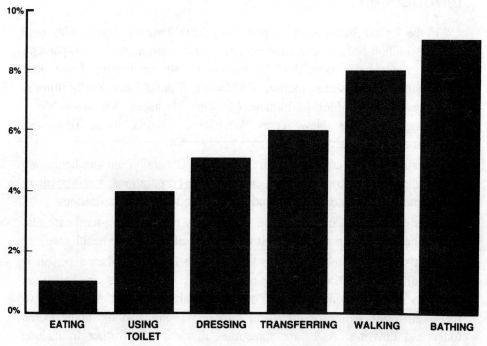

SOURCE: J. Leon and T. Lair. *Functional Status of the Noninstitutionalized Elderly: Estimates of ADL and IADL Difficulties.* DHHS Pub. No. (PHS)90-3462 (June 1990). *National Medical Expenditure Survey Research Findings* 4, Agency for Health Care Policy and Research, Rockville, MD: Public Health Service.

To receive assistance from the government (Medicare or Medicaid), or even private health insurance or HMOs, there are strict rules governing home health care. The care must be ordered by a doctor and administered by a registered nurse, licensed practical nurse or a medically trained rehabilitation therapist (such as a physical, speech or nutritional therapist). In addition to a doctor's prescription, the purpose of the care often must qualify as skilled care, as defined by Medicare. To summarize, in order to qualify as skilled care, the following must be met:

1. You must be homebound.

2. You must be under the care of a physician and have a plan of care signed by the physician.

3. You must need part-time or intermittent home health care services.

4. The care must be provided by an agency certified by Medicare.

The following table summarizes which tasks are performed most by caregivers.

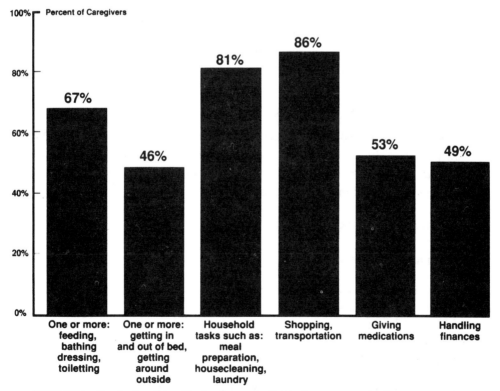

SOURCE: *1992 Long-Term Care Survey/Informal Caregivers Survey, as found in Select Committee on Aging, U.S. House of Representatives.* Exploding the Myths: Caregiving in America, *January 1987.*

Most of the tasks performed by caregivers are not considered skilled care and therefore would not be covered by Medicare. *However, Medicare will cover care of a personal or custodial nature, such as help with bathing or dressing, only if you are also under a skilled care plan.*

Paying for home health care can be expensive. You should try every possible government agency, including Medicare and Medicaid, to pay for this care. Often doctors, social workers and many home health care providers themselves do not know the scope of what Medicaid will pay.

When searching for a home health care provider, look for a Medicare-Certified Home Health Agency (CHHA). These providers are the ones Medicare has certified. Medicare reimburses the CHHA only if it determines that you are qualified for care. As a result, you may have to convince a CHHA to accept you as a patient. A CHHA may provide you with some of the care you request and then you will be responsible for the remaining care.

You should ask the CHHA to bill Medicare for the entire fee, although Medicare may deny a portion of it. However, you should submit the entire bill to Medicare anyway. You can then argue with Medicare and appeal a decision. Often it is not that difficult to appeal a Medicare decision and win.

> **It is a little known fact that Medicare has allocated roughly 2.5 percent to go toward noncovered services so CHHA can give additional care if need be.**

Where to find care providers

The following resources may help in your search for quality home health care providers. In addition to the following brief list, the Directory of Area Agencies on Aging and the list of Ombudsman Programs in the appendix are resources that should provide direction as well.

National Association for Home Care
519 C St., N.E.
Washington, DC 20002-5809

American Association of Retired Persons (AARP)
1992 rev. A Handbook About Care in the Home
AARP Fulfillment
601 E Street, NW
Washington, DC 20049

National Association of Private Geriatric Care Managers, Inc.
655 N. Alvernon Way, Suite 108
Tucson, AZ 85711
602-881-8008

In addition to needing a care provider, you may require medical equipment, such as a specific type of bed, a wheelchair, chairlift or portable toilet. Possibly your insurance company, Medicare or Medicaid will help pay for the equipment. You can also call the Social Security hotline, 1-800-772-1213 (for the hearing impaired, TDD 1-800-325-0778) to inquire about anything else you might need.

Nursing homes

Long-term care nursing homes must comply with stricter regulations than continuing care and assisted living facilities. Unfortunately, you usually enter this type of facility in an emergency fashion, when you are ill and under a great deal of stress. In fact, you have to be much more careful when you select a long-term care facility than any other type of facility.

You should bear in mind the statistics: The vast majority of people more than 85 years of age will need to spend time in a care facility. And one of the most common reasons for elderly individuals becoming impoverished in retirement is an inability to meet the costs of this long-term care. Rather than dealing with this issue, you may say, "I don't plan on giving any of my savings to my kids anyhow so why should I care what long-term care costs?" Unfortunately, you have to care about the cost because you or your spouse may still need care after all the money is spent and then you will have very few options.

Three key issues must be confronted when thinking about long-term care.

The first issue is coming to terms with the fact that this is something that is needed. You may think that it would be ideal if you would care for another family member. However, as much as you may like to, you may be physically or emotionally unable to care for someone who needs constant care. You may have your own family to care for and dealing with someone who requires attention 24 hours a day is often too much for a non-professional to handle. Also, you may not have the medical skills or equipment to care for a loved one at home.

The second concern is finding a care facility that you would be happy in or one that you feel would provide the most positive healing environment for a loved one.

The third issue is that omnipresent factor—the cost. Long-term care is a terribly expensive proposition with the average annual cost from $40,000 to $60,000 a year. In some parts of the country, you can pay up to $100,000 a year. None of the health care proposals discussed over the past few years include any provisions on long-term care cost. Few HMO and Medicare supplement policies cover long-term care, or they cover it only for a very short period of time. Medicare will probably not cover your long-term care, or if it does, it will cover it for very limited periods.

To beat the long-term care crisis, you have to adopt a strategy. The strategy is simple: Plan ahead of time, before you reach a crisis. That way, you will have a better chance of finding quality care and you'll be able to keep more of your money.

It's worth repeating the three parts of the long-term care puzzle:

1. Recognize the need.
2. Find the right care facility.
3. Determine how you'll pay for the care.

There are several kinds of nursing homes with the three most common being skilled care, intermediate care and custodial care.

Skilled care

This includes 24-hour-a-day supervision. A Registered Nurse (RN) is always on duty to administer prescription drugs, help with ADL and monitor the patients. Ironically, this is the care that is used by only .5 percent of seniors but is the care best covered by Medicare. This type of care is for seniors with major incapacitating ailments, such as severe strokes.

Intermediate care

In this type of facility, an RN may still be on duty, but the patients do not require 24-hour-a-day supervision. However, these patients do need some assistance, such as walking or performing some of the daily routine activities, such as bathing. Approximately 4.5 percent of seniors use this care.

Custodial care

This care is commonly used by seniors recovering from surgery, in the early stages of Alzheimer's, or those who cannot take care of themselves on their own. These people need help with daily routine activities. This is the care that is most used by seniors—almost 96 percent—*but is not covered by Medicare.*

You should not underestimate the significance of the subject of financing your long-term care. You are almost on your own in this area and cannot and should not rely on government assistance. The costs of nursing homes are almost overwhelming, often more than $150 per day, not including prescriptions or incidentals. *It is estimated that half of the people who enter a nursing home will face impoverishment within 13 weeks!* Are you ready to face this situation?

The American population is getting older, but it is not getting healthier with age. Since October 1993, nursing home admissions have risen by more than 42 percent. Of every dollar spent on medical costs by the elderly, according to the Senate Committee on Aging, only 19 cents are covered by Medicare. The remaining 81 cents are long-term care expenses, rarely covered by Medicare.

Finding a quality long-term care (LTC) facility

Let's first examine how you can find good quality care, then address the issue of how you will pay for it.

Some of the research you can do to find an LTC facility is similar to the research you would do if you were looking for a CCRC or an Assisted Living home. Don't hesitate to ask friends or relatives for recommendations. With so many people facing similar problems, you may find help and support from people around you.

Get help from public agencies

One excellent program that you should use is the Long-Term Care Ombudsman Program. Federal law requires each Area Agency on Aging to have an office of the Long-Term Care Ombudsman, and more than 500 local ombudsman programs now exist nationwide. These offices provide help and information to older Americans and their families regarding long-term care facilities. The Ombudsman offices usually have lists of local facilities, investigate complaints and visit local care facilities regularly. Although the Ombudsman will not recommend specific facilities to you, the office can provide you with surveys of the state facilities and has records of complaints against the facilities. (See Appendix 4 for a list of Ombudsman programs in your state.)

Each state's Health Department produces a yearly report on the performance of each nursing home that is certified for Medicare or Medicaid. Most Ombudsman offices will have this report. If there isn't an Ombudsman office near you, contact your Area Agency on Aging. You may even ask the nursing home to give you a copy of the report. Homes are required to have copies of it and you may want to review the report with the home's administrator.

Communicate your wishes to your family

You have to plan ahead for the day when you may not be able to manage on your own and express your wishes. You should ask yourself the following questions and make sure a family member knows how you feel.

1. If you can no longer live independently, where would you like to live? Do you want to move in with children? Would you prefer living in a residential care facility? Or, would you rather try to find a roommate or a companion who could look after you and provide some assistance?

2. How do you anticipate paying for these options?

3. What forms of life support and/or resuscitative measures would you want used on yourself?

Once you can answer these questions, you can begin to formulate some realistic plans for the future. Educating yourself about available services is the first step toward productive planning. But you should be aware that even the best planning will not make the decision easier if you have to place a loved one in a nursing home.

How to find the right facility

You need to evaluate several factors as you make a decision whether to place a loved one in a care facility. Does your loved one need constant 24-hour-a-day care? Could you find adequate in-home care? Remember, too, that Medicare and Medicaid coverage for in-home care tends to be very limited, with more than 50 percent of such expenses being shouldered by the families and the individuals needing care. If you need more hours of coverage than are included, and you don't have the funds to pay privately, you will probably be forced to consider placement. Are you physically capable of caring for a loved one full-time?

After you have determined that you are unable to care for your relative at home, you can begin to search for the best facility for him or her. Begin by listing all the facilities—both privately owned for profit and nonprofit—in the geographic region you prefer. However, you should be aware that because of the increasing number of older people and the advancements in medical technology that can sustain life, fewer nursing homes are being built. This means that there may not be enough beds available in your community to accommodate all the people who need to be in a nursing home. Therefore, you may need to be more flexible when you compile your list of acceptable facilities. The facility you ultimately choose may not be the one most conveniently located.

You must also understand how money determines your options when selecting a nursing home. Paying for private nursing home care is very expensive, up to $60,000 a year in some regions. And this figure may not include other expenses such as medications or physicians' visits. In most states the majority of nursing home residents are subsidized by Medicaid. Unlike Medicare, which covers care in skilled nursing facilities for specified conditions and time allotments, Medicaid covers the cost of this care for eligible persons for as long as their condition requires it. However, the facilities that accept Medicaid will often do so only after an individual has paid privately for a period of time. With the costs of care so high, it is understandable that most people entering private nursing homes will exhaust their resources in a relatively short time period. If you or a relative is in a lower income bracket, you will probably be eligible for, and rely on, Medicaid to pay for nursing home expenses. If your assets are sufficient to allow you to pay for long-term care, you have several choices. You can use those assets but risk depleting them—which is especially dangerous if you have a spouse living at home—or you can purchase long-term care insurance to help pay for this care.

Once you have narrowed down your search to include those facilities that provide the level of care you or your relative needs, and whose financial requirements you can meet, you can begin to evaluate each facility you're considering. Try to visit each facility on several occasions at different times of the day. You should observe the staff in action. Look at their attitude toward the residents. Is the staff concerned about the residents? Are bedridden residents attended to frequently or do they seem to be forgotten about in their rooms?

Look into several residents' rooms to see how much space each one has. Is space so tight that it is difficult for a resident with a walker or a cane to move safely around the room? Can a wheelchair be easily maneuvered? These factors are important in considering how independent a resident can be. Of course, you want to check if the room is clean and fresh-smelling. Try to visit during dining hours to see if most of the residents eat in a central dining room and can socialize. Or are most of the residents fed in their rooms? Are activities geared for the more frail as well as the more capable residents? The more facilities you visit, the better a basis for comparison you will have. The transition to nursing home life is difficult for everyone involved, so you should feel that you have done your best to select the facility most appropriate to your particular situation.

You can use the following checklist to help you evaluate a nursing home facility:

Checklist to evaluate a nursing home

Administrative factors

- Is the facility currently licensed and accredited?

- Is the nursing home certified for participation in the Medicare or Medicaid programs?

- Are the findings of the most recent inspection posted?

- What are the facility's admissions requirements for residents?

- Does the nursing home require that a resident sign over personal property or real estate in exchange for care?

- Does the facility have any vacancies or is there a waiting list?

- Is the administrator of the facility licensed?

- Does the facility have a medical director? If so, how active is he or she in the day-to-day operation of the facility?

- Is the facility clean and relatively free of odor?

- What is the visitors' policy?

- How many beds are in each room? (Four should be the maximum.)

Fees

- Is a deposit required on admission? Is there a refund policy if the resident leaves the facility or dies?

- Is the facility eligible for Medicare and Medicaid reimbursement?

- What does the basic rate cover? What services are extra and billed separately?

- Will your insurance policy cover any of the charges?

Staff

- Is there a doctor on call 24 hours a day?

- What is the nurse/resident ratio on each shift?

- Do professional specialists including dentists, podiatrists, ophthalmologists and audiologists regularly visit the facility?

- How often is diagnostic work such as cardiograms, x-rays and laboratory testing performed?

- How often are rehabilitative services including physical therapy, occupational therapy and speech therapy provided?

- Does the nursing staff provide restorative programs—basic exercises and ambulating to those residents who do not require the services of a professional therapist?

- Is a social worker available to assist residents and their families?

- Does the staff provide an orientation program to help both residents and family members to adjust to life in the facility?

- Is the staff friendly and efficient? If possible, ask several residents how they feel about the atmosphere in the facility.

- What is the training and experience of the nurses? Do they seem caring to you? Can you communicate well with them? Do you think they will make the right decisions in an emergency situation?

- Do the residents appear to be alert and involved in their surroundings, or do they appear to be overmedicated or restrained?

Food

- Are the meals balanced, well-prepared and appetizingly presented?

- Do residents eat in a communal dining room or do they dine in their rooms?

- Is feeding assistance provided promptly to those residents who need it?

- Are special meals available for the residents with dietary problems?

Activities

- Are activities offered regularly throughout the day, seven days a week?

- Is there an active volunteer program? Are community volunteers welcomed enthusiastically?

- Are activities designed for the special needs of all residents regardless of their functional ability or limitations?

- Are there field trips, guest speakers and other events scheduled each month?

- Is there an active Residents Council? This allows the residents to have input into the management of the facility.

Attitude toward residents

- Are residents treated with dignity and respect, or are they spoken to as if they were children?

- Do residents have privacy when they're dressing, bathing or visiting?

- Are residents encouraged to bring personal belongings? Is a homey atmosphere encouraged?

- Are there arrangements for regular religious observance?

- Are a barber and beautician available regularly?

Residents' rights

Working in a nursing home can be very demanding. Physically you may have to transport and even restrain patients. In addition, many of the companies that operate nursing homes are trying to boost their profitability, which results in understaffing and/or staffing nonqualified nurses' aids. Unfortunately, these problems can lead to neglect and abuse.

Patient abuse and neglect was the impetus for enactment of the Nursing Home Reform Act, as part of the 1987 Omnibus Budget Reform Act (OBRA 87). This led to what is known as the Nursing Home Resident's Bill of Rights. The premise is that "a resident has a right to a dignified existence, self-determination, and communication with access to provisions and services inside and outside the facility." Furthermore, a "care facility must promote care for residents in a manner and in an environment that maintains or enhances each resident's dignity and respect in full recognition of his or her individuality."

To receive payments, nursing homes must be Medicare-certified institutions. To be certified, the institution must follow certain rules and regulations pertaining to the care of the facilities' residents. In addition to following the set of guidelines, there will be at least one on-site inspection a year. These inspections are usually unannounced, and the review is quite lengthy. The review covers such issues as residents' rights, admission transfer and discharge rights, resident behavior and facility practices, quality of life, resident assessment, quality of care, nursing services, dietary services, physician services, specialized rehabilitation services, dental services, pharmacy service, infection control and physical environment.

Each time a facility does not meet federal standards the facility will be cited as being deficient. Then the nursing home must adopt a plan of correction for each deficiency. Further, a survey report (From HCFA 2567) entitled "Statement of Deficiencies and Plan of Correction" is completed to summarize the results of each survey in which the surveyors locate deficiencies. The resulting report from the inspection is required by law to be posted, in plain view, somewhere in the nursing home.

> **Always read the finding from the survey
> prior to being admitted to a nursing home.**

If you want to review all the surveys of the facilities near you, contact your local Ombudsman office and ask for a list. These surveys provide a wealth of information that will help guide you in the search for a sound facility.

If a nursing home does not participate in the Medicare or Medicaid programs, it still must be licensed in the state in which it operates. Unfortunately there is no uniform state nursing home licensing law. Usually, however, the state rules will follow the federal nursing home law, and some states have stricter laws.

The nursing home admission process

The admission process for nursing homes is tricky, to say the least. Not only do you have to make sure that the home is right for you, the home will want to make sure you are right for the facility. This is why it's important that you evaluate care facilities well in advance of a crisis. If you wait until a crisis, the cards will be stacked against you. You may not get into the facility of your choice, or you may be forced to pay much more than you would otherwise. Remember, many facilities are completely occupied and have waiting lists.

The nursing home will evaluate you on two main factors:

1. What is your need and can the facility accommodate that need?

2. How much money do you have?

Studies from the United States Government Accounting Office say that reasons individuals have difficulty gaining admittance to care facilities include already having Medicaid and mental or behavioral problems.

One of the strictest Medicaid rules states that in order for a nursing home to be a Medicaid-approved facility, the facility is not allowed to discharge a resident who is a private payer simply because he or she runs out of money. Instead the care facility must accept that patient under Medicaid. This means that if you go in as a private payer (or because you have long-term care insurance), and then subsequently spend all your money, you will not be booted out of that particular care facility (so long as the facility is Medicare-approved). As a result of this rule, care institutions are particular about how much money you have. They would rather have private payers than Medicaid recipients, because the facility can charge the private payers more than what Medicaid pays them. In addition, a private-pay resident is charged based on the care needed (such as light care, special care, etc.), while the Medicaid pay rate is the same for all recipients regardless of the care. If you call a care facility and tell them you are on Medicaid and ask if there is room for you, chances are there will not be any room. On the other hand, if you say you are a private payer, your chances for admittance are much greater.

> **It is for this reason that I always recommend that people try to gain admittance as private payers, and then apply for Medicaid.**

When you complete the admission form, you should be very careful about revealing your financial assets. If you write down that you have all these assets, you will be at a disadvantage if you want to apply for Medicaid in the future. Medicaid will ask you what happened to all your assets. If Medicaid determines that you have given away assets within the "look-back period," you might not be eligible for Medicaid.

Many individuals are admitted to care facilities under a third party, such as an adult son or daughter. The important question is, "What is the legal relationship between the nursing home, the applicant and the third party?" If the son or daughter state that he or she will be paying for their sick parent's care, and then stop paying for the care, does the nursing facility have any recourse? Is the facility obligated to allow the sick resident continued care under Medicaid?

> **This is one strategy certain individuals employ: A person will gain admittance to a care facility as a private payer, paid by a third party (child or relative), and then the third party stops paying. Medicaid then continues the support.**

Most states do not have legal support agreements in place. This means the third party has no legal obligation to their relative. The main exception to this rule would be among spouses who do have a legal obligation for support.

What to look for in the admission agreement

Prior to entering a care facility, you will be required to sign an admissions agreement. You need to read carefully through this lengthy and difficult document to determine if you will be getting the care that you expect to receive. The following is a list of things you should find out before signing the document.

1. Know what the per-diem rate includes. If you are on Medicare or Medicaid, the Health Care Financing Administration has decided what is included in the per-diem rate. You can get from your local Medicaid office a specific list of what is included. (See appendix for an office near you.) The following are a few of the basic items that are almost always included in the per-diem rate:

   - Room and board.
   - Nursing services.
   - Therapeutic and rehabilitation services.
   - Activities program.
   - Medically related social services.
   - For Medicaid, routine personal hygiene items.

   If you are not on Medicare or Medicaid, most states do not have a cap on the per-diem rate. In addition, the rate is subject to regular increases. You should ask for a specific list of what is included and what factors determine when your rate would increase. Try to get a guarantee that the care facility will not raise your rate for a set number of years.

2. Understand the payment terms if you are a private payer. You should find out if you have to continually pay six months in advance, or if you can pay on a monthly basis. If you pay a deposit (as most care facilities require), is it refundable? There have been some unscrupulous nursing home administrators who have tried to control the assets of the patients and refuse to return these deposits. In some cases, a resident must make a deposit that he or she agrees to pay as a private payer prior to converting to a Medicaid recipient. This is called "duration of stay" and is not legal. On average, anything over two months of the per-diem rate as a deposit is excessive. If the resident should die prior to using the deposit, it should be refunded.

3. Though not required by law, the admission contract should include a restatement of your rights as a resident. You also want to make sure that nothing in the contract takes rights away from you.

   A resident has a right to refuse any heroic or life-sustaining measures. (See the sample living will in this text.) Examples would include CPR, IV tubes for nutrition, calling for emergency services, ventilators, kidney dialysis, etc. A resident can reject any portion of his or her plan for treatment. A resident should never be asked to sign a blanket statement giving consent to a care facility to do anything the facility wishes for your medical treatment.

4. Be aware of your discharge rights as a patient. As a result of OBRA 87, a nursing home can not discharge private-pay residents if their money runs out. The only exceptions would be if the resident got better, if the resident deteriorated so much the nursing home could not provide adequate medical care or if the resident endangered the health or safety of other residents or staff.

Summary

When searching for a nursing home, it's important to do your homework. It's easy to fall into traps, such as paying too much to get a home when you might qualify for government aid, or selecting a facility that requires turning over some assets in order to be admitted. It is important that you carefully weigh a variety of factors, including the location, staff and care, as well as the cost. Since nursing homes are expensive, you should look into government assistance. A positive nursing home experience can be a wonderful way to ease your pain or the discomfort of a loved one. Or it could be a terrible experience, because of poor facilities, abuse, high costs, etc. You should thoroughly evaluate care facilities in order to make the experience a positive one for you or a loved one.

Chapter 8

How to pay for long-term care

Advance planning is crucial

To repeat what cannot be emphasized enough: long-term care can wipe you out if you don't plan ahead financially, as well as emotionally. Most people define planning as "crisis planning." In other words, when a problem arises, you decide to fix it at that moment. For example, your mother just had a stroke, so you will immediately need to make some decisions. You have to find a good facility with an available bed, protect your money and maintain your sanity at the same time. Most likely, you won't be able to handle these decisions simultaneously. Crisis planning is the worst way to plan. True planning is "proactive planning." You plan ahead for what you would do in the event something happens in the future. Unfortunately, you're likely to get into trouble because of the "p" words. You *procrastinate*, and as a result don't *plan*. This could develop into a major problem—*poverty*.

The following are the reasons why it is essential to plan ahead of time how to pay for long-term care.

- If you spend all your money on care costs, but then recover and are well again, you will have no resources available to pay for your day-to-day living expenses.

- If all your money is used to pay for a sick spouse, you will not have any resources for your living expenses.

- There will be no money remaining to leave as an inheritance for your children or grandchildren.

- You wouldn't want to be a burden on your family.

- You will have fewer choices about where you receive your long-term care if you have no funds available and are forced to go on Medicaid immediately.

You should realize, therefore, that you must determine ahead of time how you will cover your long-term care expenses. There are five major ways to pay for this care.

Ways to pay for long-term care costs

1. Private pay: You pay on your own from savings and with assistance from your family.

2. Medicare, Medicare supplements and other assistance programs used to the maximum.

3. Private insurance and hybrid insurance plans mixed with public benefits.

4. Public benefits including Medicaid.

5. Cost reduction strategies such as sharing costs, etc.

Private care, private pay—moving level to level

You're not alone if you feel that, if you can afford it, you should pay for your own care. While this philosophy sounds fine in theory, very few people can afford this burden over an extended period of time. Assume that the care will cost $40,000. In addition, you need to calculate other expenses such as extra rehabilitation and the living expenses of the well spouse. And, if the well spouse ends up getting sick, you will need even more funds. A vast amount of money will be spent in a very short period of time.

Still, if you are determined to save money for private long-term care, you will have to start a savings program long before you might need it. It's not too soon to begin planning while you're in your 20s or 30s. When you calculate how much money you will need for retirement, include enough money to cover five to seven years of long-term care for you and your spouse.

When you are using your own funds to pay for long-term care costs, make sure that you do not overpay. Ask that you get the best possible rates. Make sure that you pay only for services that will not be covered by Medicare or other insurance coverage. Check into all the government programs for which you may be eligible. Even if you have saved to pay for your long-term care, you should still take advantage of any funds or other services available from government agencies.

Long-term care insurance

When long-term care insurance was first introduced, some people were skeptical. The concept seemed valid but there was little regulation and no one knew if the insurers would in fact pay the benefits.

There are many valid reasons to look into LTC insurance. With the aging population and the number of users of LTC continuing to increase, more people are going to go broke, there will be a reduction in entitlement programs and higher taxes to support these programs. The bottom line is that things are going to get very messy.

This is not the place to debate whether you think the government owes you and should pay for your time in a LTC facility. Assume that it is extremely difficult to get the government to pay for your care (see Medicaid sections of this text) in spite of the high odds that you will use a LTC facility. Therefore, you should try to find an insurance policy that will provide coverage for long-term care at a fair price. If you can find such a policy, then long-term care insurance is worth getting.

Although there are now many ways of buying insurance, the costs are still high. Furthermore, because people tend to procrastinate so long, the insurance will probably be bought late in life (after age 65), which is, of course, the age when the costs of the insurance begin to rise dramatically.

When you investigate long-term care insurance, there are many questions that you need to ask.

Questions to ask before purchasing long-term care insurance

How is the policy underwriting performed?

Some companies will perform the underwriting immediately upon your application and determine if you are accepted or not before allowing you to pay a premium. Once accepted, many of these companies will maintain your coverage even if subsequent investigations uncover some reason why you shouldn't have gotten the coverage.

Other companies will accept you but will do their underwriting only after you file a claim or get sick. If the insurer finds errors on your application, it will deny your claim. Let's assume on your application you were asked if you had any heart problems in the last five years. You thought the last time you had heart problems was six years ago, so you answer the question with a no. However, your last heart problem was, in fact, within the past five years. The company may be able to deny you coverage. Other companies will put a time limit, usually two years, in the policy for their underwriting. This means if the insurance company finds errors on your application two or more years after you were issued the policy, it will remain in effect and your coverage will not change.

What determines whether your claim for long-term care benefits will be honored? What conditions must you meet in order to qualify for the insurance benefits?

This is an extremely difficult question to answer. Some insurance companies will pay if you simply cannot perform two out of five of the activities of daily living (see the long-term care section). If you need assistance eating and bathing, you deserve benefits. Other insurance companies are stricter and require that you need help in three, four or even five different daily living activities.

Also, policies vary in specifying whose opinion is used to determine whether you can or cannot perform a daily living activity. In some cases your doctor's opinion is sufficient, but other policies require you to be examined by a doctor appointed by the insurance company.

Will you be covered only if you come directly from a hospital?

While most LTC insurance policies do not require you to come directly from a hospital in order to receive coverage, some do. You should avoid such a provision because, often, many illnesses such as Alzheimer's are gradual and will not require a hospital stay.

How can the company raise your premiums?

There are three different types of premiums:

- A *level* premium is usually defined as a fixed premium that will not go up or down.

- A *gradual* premium increases periodically, according to stipulations in your policy such as age or medical condition.

- A *lump-sum* premium refers to an amount that is required in a one-time deposit to pay-up the policy.

Although many companies will tout a "guaranteed annual renewable" policy, this simply means the company cannot cancel your contract. It does not mean that the company will not increase your premiums. Ask whether the increases are capped; this means your increases cannot exceed a certain amount. Can the premiums increase as you age or if your health deteriorates?

Is there an inflation protection clause?

Hopefully, it will be many years before you will have to enter a nursing home. If you purchase insurance that will cover you for $100 per day in daily benefits—adequate coverage if you enter a nursing home today—what happens 10 years from now when the average cost per day is $150? For this reason, you should consider purchasing inflation protection.

Inflation protection comes in two forms: simple and compounded benefits. With a simple inflation rider, your premium is usually tied to the CPI index or a flat percentage, possibly 4 percent, every year, based on the original amount purchased (assume $100). The compound benefit will increase every year with the CPI index or a straight percentage, but on the higher amount every year.

The table below illustrates how inflation could seriously and adversely impact the cost of a long-term stay. For example, if inflation averages 5 percent, and the average cost per day in a nursing home is $100, by the year 2000, the cost would increase to about $163 per day, and by 2010, the cost would be astronomically high at $265 per day.

As you can see, inflation protection should be considered when you're researching policies. If you buy coverage based on a $100 daily benefit, but you don't need the care for another 10 years, you might not have adequate protection.

Average daily rates for nursing home care

Inflation rate	1990	2000	2010
5%	$100	$163	$265
6%	$100	$179	$321
7%	$100	$197	$387
8%	$100	$216	$466

You should carefully assess the costs. The compound benefit is preferable but quite costly. If the simple benefit is included, that might be a better alternative.

When do benefits start and how long will they last?

When benefits begin is usually referred to as the "elimination period." The elimination period is the length of time you would have to be responsible for payments before your insurance starts paying. Most companies offer elimination periods ranging from immediate benefits up to a three-month waiting period. Which elimination period you choose has a direct impact on the cost of the policy.

Most people use long-term care facilities for short-term duration. If you get a lengthy elimination period, you may not be realizing the full benefits. However, the cost of the premium for immediate benefits is incredibly high.

For example, assume you wanted to buy long-term care insurance and wanted your benefits to begin immediately upon entering a nursing home. Assume that this policy will cost you $1,500 a year. However, if you bought a similar policy with benefits beginning three months after you are admitted into a nursing home, you would have to pay all the costs for those first three months. If the costs are $3,000 per month, you would be responsible for paying $9,000. However, your premium for this policy might only be $1,000 annually.

Ask the company if the benefit is cumulative. Let's assume that your elimination period is three months. In January 1995, you go into a nursing home and spend three months in the facility. In November of the same year you re-enter the facility. Will the insurance pay from day one since you have already used the three-month elimination period or does the elimination period start over? Most companies say the elimination period is cumulative per year and then starts again the next year. So, if you only use three months in a facility in 1995, in 1996, you will need to pay the first three months again, prior to receiving your insurance benefit. Remember, every carrier is different. Read your policy carefully and make sure the agent puts everything he or she has promised in writing. Then, call the insurance company yourself to verify your understanding of the elimination period rules.

What is the rating of the insurance company?

The quality of the insurance company is very important and should be evaluated in several ways. The traditional method is to look at the ratings. This is important because, chances are, the higher the rating, the greater the solvency of the company (the chance the company will be around). *A.M. Best* offers a highest rating of A++ Superior; *Standard and Poor's* and *Moody's* offers a highest rating of AAA. Ratings guides are generally available at local libraries. Although ratings are important, they should not be the only criteria you use when evaluating the quality of a company.

One very useful exercise is to call the company several times. Is there a toll-free number? Each time you call back, ask for various departments. Do you get the answers you want? Call up and pretend you are a policy holder who needs to file a claim. See how helpful the company operators are and whether the customer service representatives are familiar with the necessary procedures.

Another evaluation technique is to ask for the company's *claims paying ratio*. Ask for this ratio in writing. This ratio is extremely important because it tells you what percentage of filed claims are paid by the insurer. If the company gets 100 requests for claims, and they only pay 50, that means the company's claims paying ratio is only 50 percent. In other words, you have a 50/50 chance of receiving compensation if you file a claim. Recent studies show that the average probability that you will not receive benefits ranges as high as 50 percent to 60 percent.

When and to whom will benefits be paid?

As you can imagine, at this critical time, you need your money promptly. From the time you file a claim, how long does the company have to respond or send a check? Does the insurer have three months to evaluate the claim and decide if you are covered? Or does the company need to make a decision and cut you a check within one week?

Some insurance companies will pay the benefit directly to the care facility. However, you should have the benefit paid directly to you or a conservator if you are sick. If your policy stipulates a $100 per day benefit, and you find a facility that costs $80, then you will want to get the full benefit, pay the facility and do whatever you want with the remaining $20.

What types of care are included?

The most comprehensive policy will offer coverage for all three types of care facilities (custodial, intermediate and skilled care). Many policies will either offer or have coverage in a rider for a variety of other care including home health care, adult day care and respite care.

Again, you will need to find out specifically what it would take to receive the home health care benefit and how much per day you would receive. Make the following specific queries:

- Will you pay for non-medical needs such as someone to come in and groom the patient or run errands?
- Will you pay for equipment in the home?
- Will you modify the home by putting in rails or whatever else is needed?

Adult day care is also another excellent idea. Imagine a well spouse who takes care of an early-stage Alzheimer's spouse. The well spouse is the caregiver; he or she needs time to run errands, exercise or simply get a break from caregiving. Adult day care lets a caregiver drop off the spouse for an hour, a day or other period of time.

Typically there are two types of adult day care programs; one is medically-based and the other is recreational-oriented. The medically-based programs usually provide occupational and physical therapy services for the sick. Certain facilities even offer special services, depending on the condition such as stroke or Alzheimer's. The recreational programs focus more on activities for the person attending the day care center such as games, exercise, arts and crafts, etc.

Just like child day care, this service is valuable but expensive. As a result, many policies cover this care.

Respite care is often used for the person who will be in a facility for a short period of time, probably recuperating from an illness or an operation. Some adult day care facilities actually have respite care on the premises.

How much per day benefit should you get?

The policies that you will review will generally offer daily benefits averaging between $80 and $100. This seems reasonable based on the average costs of nursing home stays. However, if you feel you can bear the burden of a portion of the cost, tailor the policy to meet your needs. Also, you should decide if you want the inflation rider.

Some policies will pay the average cost of care in your area. This is not your best option. Too much confusion is possible because of the different costs of facilities in different locations.

Who chooses the facility?

Do you have full discretion to choose the facility you want to live in or does the insurance company have to approve the institution? Does the insurer require the facility have certain credentials and licenses? Does the facility have to be Medicare approved?

Is the policy guaranteed renewable?

This means that once you have been accepted, no matter what illnesses you suffer later, you are guaranteed the right to continue your policy as long as you live.

In addition to making certain that the policy is guaranteed renewable, find out what the lapse period is before your policy is canceled. For example, if you pay your premium 30 days late, will your policy be canceled? Are there special provisions should you become ill, possibly mentally ill, and forget to pay the premium? Are there remedies in this situation? You should name someone to be notified if your premium payment is excessively late. That way, the person can contact you or pay the premium if necessary.

Does the policy have nonforfeiture options?

Some people are firmly convinced they will never get sick, others cannot afford premiums any longer, while still others feel that they would rather take a vacation than worry about their possible future medical needs.

It would be a shame if you paid premiums for many years and then either stopped paying or passed on without receiving any benefit. To compensate you, insurers have several different nonforfeiture options. Some companies offer a benefit whereby, even if you stop paying premiums, you are guaranteed one month of benefits for every year your premium was paid. If you paid the policy premiums for 10 years, then canceled the policy, you would always be guaranteed 10 months of benefits under a "nonforfeiture" clause. This means, if you paid the policy premiums for 10 years and then canceled the policy, you would always be guaranteed 10 months of benefits.

When evaluating the benefits of this type of policy, you should weight the benefits purely on the costs. If a policy with a nonforfeiture option costs you $1,500 per year, and you paid for 10 years, you would have spent $15,000. If you now stop paying, assume the policy gives you 10 months of benefits. If the nursing home costs you $3,000 per month, the policy benefit is $30,000.

Assume you purchased the same policy without the nonforfeiture option. The premium is $1,200. You pay this for 10 years and spend $12,000. But, you take the $300 that you saved on the policy each year and invest it, earning an 8 percent return. At the end of 10 years, you would have saved about $4,500. If you cancel the policy after 10 years, you will have no nursing home benefits. The $4,500 that you were able to save on the reduced premium does not come close to the benefit of the policy with the nonforfeiture option in this example.

Another option is a death benefit that is paid if you have not used a portion of benefits for long-term care.

Be savvy before purchasing a policy

Do your homework and of course, call each one of the companies. This will help your search a great deal. You should also contact the state insurance commissioner. This office will probably be able to give you advice or lead you in the right direction to an advocacy group. You should also contact the National Association of Insurance Commissioners (NAIC; 444 N. Capital St. NW, Washington, DC 20001-1512; 202-624-7790) for guidance as well. Another excellent resource is the National Insurance Consumer Helpline (800-942-4242). This group is sponsored by the insurance industry and can answer questions about life, disability and long-term care insurance.

Partnership for Long-Term Care

A few states including California and Connecticut have begun a program called the Partnership for Long-Term Care in conjunction with a federal grant through the Robert Wood Johnson Foundation, State Insurance Commissioners and selected insurance companies. The program's premise is to provide long-term care benefits without forcing people to go broke. The concept works as follows: Let's assume you have a net worth of $150,000, and are afraid of going broke should you need long-term care. So you purchase a policy for long-term care to cover $150,000 worth of benefits. After your $150,000 of benefits is used up, Medicaid would pay the next $150,000 without you having to lose all your money to qualify. The rules vary from state to state. The concept is a good one, and you should contact your insurance commissioner to see if your state has a similar program. However, this is a pilot program and will last only for a limited period of time. What is uncertain is whether your benefits will be grandfathered if Medicaid changes its rules. It's not clear if you can't qualify for Medicaid, whether you will still get the Medicaid benefits before having to "spend-down" your assets.

Assured care

This is quite unique coverage. This type of insurance is really life insurance with a twist; you can use the life insurance death benefit or a specified portion of the policy to pay for long-term care expenses. Are the policies any good? It depends on the policy and the cost. You should determine the exact benefit you will receive as insurance and/or long-term care benefits. Then, figure how much it would cost you to buy a long-term care insurance policy and a straight life insurance policy, or simply take the extra money to "self-insure" yourself.

For example, assume you are considering putting $25,000 in a single premium assured care policy. The policy has a death benefit of $60,000, which you can also use to pay for long-term care costs. You give the insurance company $25,000 and your beneficiaries will get $60,000 if you die. So, technically the true amount of insurance is $35,000 ($25,000 was already your money). The same is true for long-term care benefits.

On the other hand, if you took your $25,000 and bought a long-term care policy giving you $60,000 in benefits, you would pay roughly $1,500 per year. Assume that you could invest the $20,000, earn an 8% return and pay the $1,500 premium from the $20,000. In 15 years you would have roughly $35,000. Basically the insurance for long-term care would not cost you anything, and your money would grow by about $15,000. You must decide which is the better option—the life insurance or the cash.

A few other considerations will also impact your decision. The cash value buildup of a life insurance policy is tax-free until you pull the money out. If the money is used to pay for long-term care, is it considered cash value or the death benefit? How is the money taxed? Is it considered income in the year you pay long-term care costs? If it is and you use the money to pay long-term care costs, where will you come up with the money to pay taxes?

One other important point to consider is whether you will try to receive Medicaid benefits at a later date to pay long-term care costs. Medicaid only allows you to have a limited amount in cash value and in insurance; currently, you can have $1,500 in cash value in an insurance policy. If you have more in cash value, you may not receive Medicaid benefits. Also, if you have insurance proceeds available to pay long-term care costs, you will probably not have a choice whether to use the death benefit of the insurance. You will probably have to use the insurance for long-term care before you can receive any type of government assistance.

Summary

Once you recognize that you or a loved one needs to enter a long-term care facility, there are two crucial steps you must take: You must select the best facility for your needs and you must figure out how to pay for the care. There are several ways to pay for long-term care. Probably, you will use a combination of the following sources: private insurance, government assistance, special care arrangements and savings. Don't assume that you will qualify for Medicare and Medicaid without researching the eligibility requirements. You should gather all the relevant information and assess your options. If you choose to buy long-term care insurance, you must review the policy carefully. Not only must you look at the present premium cost, but what the policy is likely to cost in the years ahead. In addition, you must find out what types of care are covered under your policy, whether you or the insurer chooses the facility, whether the policy is automatically renewable, etc. Don't choose the wrong policy in haste without reviewing every clause.

Chapter 9

Paying for long-term care and home health care, part II

The basics of Medicare

Medicare is part of the Social Security Act, a federal entitlement program. It provides basic medical benefits for most insured workers at age 65. Chances are if you qualify for Social Security benefits, you qualify for Medicare. You might even qualify for Medicare without being fully insured through Social Security. (For a detailed discussion of Medicare, read my book, *The Complete Guide to Social Security*.)

The premise of Medicare is to provide a medically needed service that will help stabilize a patient. Currently, the Medicare program is being hotly debated in Washington and some legislators are calling for a drastic overhaul of the entire program. Already, because of cost containment measures, Medicare is paying much less than in the past. If you had a hip replacement operation in 1990, you would probably have stayed in the hospital until you were well. Today, you are sent home as soon as you are "stabilized." You have two choices: You can go to a custodial type of facility where you can get help with the activities of daily living until you are well, or you can go home and have someone come help you. Either way, Medicare will probably not approve your condition as a "medical need" and you will have to pay out of your pocket.

What's particularly frightening is that if you get sick or have an accident, you'll be unprepared, trying to make arrangements at the last minute and not knowing who to contact. Imagine you're the victim of a stroke. After your vital signs have stabilized and you are released from the hospital, then what happens? You're not ready to drive, walk, groom yourself or run errands.

Unfortunately Medicare is not designed to pay for long-term care costs. It contains a provision to pay a certain dollar amount for a very short time, usually a maximum of 100 days of benefits. First, you must meet the basic requirements before you get any Medicare payments:

1. Medicare only pays if you are in a skilled nursing facility.

2. Your skilled nursing home visit must be preceded by a hospital stay of at least three days.

3. The nursing home must meet the Medicare standard of coverage and be certified under Medicare.

These are difficult criteria to meet. Most people don't use skilled care facilities. Most long-term care stays are custodial care, respite, etc. Secondly, many of the people in nursing homes don't precede their nursing home stay by a three-day hospital visit. Finally, many of the individuals in nursing homes remain there longer than 100 days, which is more than the number of days that Medicare will cover.

One important point that you shouldn't overlook is the "preceding hospital stay." Although you may have been in the hospital for three days, *you might not be covered if you go to a care facility, because you were not registered in the hospital correctly.* Sometimes people stay in hospitals longer than expected and are never admitted: Your records may list you as an "outpatient" even if you stayed in the hospital. Although you were there three days, Medicare is not obligated to recognize that as a hospital stay. As a result, you could be denied coverage if you go directly to a skilled nursing home and meet all other applicable requirements. Because of these limitations, Medicare only pays for roughly 2 percent of all the persons that are in Medicare facilities today.

If you think you qualify for Medicare benefits, fill out the proper application available at your local Social Security office. Or you can call the toll-free hotline for Social Security and Medicare at 800-772-1213.

If you are turned down for coverage, but believe you are entitled to it, appeal the decision. Appeals shouldn't cost you anything, possibly only a minimal amount, and are worth trying. In fact, senior citizens are entitled to certain legal benefits and some organizations (see Appendix) might help represent you for no fee or nominal charges.

Once you are in a long-term care facility, there will probably be many services you will receive that are covered under Medicare. Review closely or have someone else review your bills and what you are paying for. Many medical services are covered under Medicare part A, and still others are covered under part B, including the cost of equipment, therapy and certain medications. Don't pay if Medicare should be paying, and make sure you are not being billed for services billed to Medicare. See the charts on pages 88, 89, 90 and 91 to get an idea of what Medicare pays for and what your costs are.

The key to using Medicare is to first find out if you have received coverage. See if you would be covered under the Qualified Medicare Beneficiary Program (QMB).

Medicare supplements, Health Maintenance Organizations (HMOs)

Medicare only pays for selected medical services, and you are responsible for the deductibles and copayments of these.

When you're choosing a Medicare supplement insurance plan (Medi-Gap plan), whether it is a private insurance plan or Health Maintenance Organization (HMO), you should find out exactly which long-term care costs it will cover. Ask the insurer specific questions about your Medicare supplement or HMO such as:

1. Does the company pay for nutrition programs, Meals on Wheels, etc.?

2. Is any home care covered? What is required to receive coverage and how much will be covered? Which of the activities of daily living are part of the requirements for this coverage?

3. Will the company pay for nonmedical types of care such as help with grooming, dressing or meal preparation?

4. What requirements must be met to receive payment for services such as adult day care, respite care, etc.?

5. If the company pays for any type of long-term care from custodial to home care, how much of the cost is covered and for how long?

Other programs to help cut medical costs

Medicare has two special programs for qualified beneficiaries. The first program is known as the Qualified Medicare Beneficiary Program (QMB). This program pays part A and part B premiums, as well as deductibles and co-insurance expenses. The strict qualification rules depend on where you live. The general guideline is that you must have income at or below national poverty levels and also your current assets must be below poverty guidelines as well.

MEDICARE PART A:
MEDICAL INSURANCE

Service	Medicare Benefits	Your Cost
Hospitalization	Full cost after deductible is met (1st-60th day)	$652 per benefit period in 1992
	Full cost after co-insurance (61st-90th day)	$163 per day co-insurance in 1992
	Full cost after co-insurance for 60 lifetime reserve days, OR	$326 per day co-insurance in 1992
	$0 after 60 reserve days are used.	Full cost
Post-hospital care in a certified skilled-nursing facility (SNF)	100% of approved amounts for the first 20 days of care each benefit period after 3-day hospital stay	$0
	Full cost after co-insurance (21st-100th day)	$81.50 per day co-insurance in 1992
	$0 after 100th day	Full cost
Intermediate and custodial nursing care	$0	Full cost
Home health care	100% of approved amount of Medicare-approved services	$0
	80% of approved amount for durable medical equipment	20% of approved amount in 1992
Hospice	All but limited costs for outpatient drugs and inpatient respite care	Limited cost-sharing for outpatient drugs and inpatient respite care
Blood	Full cost after first 3 pints	First 3 pints

The second program is known as the Specified Low Income Medicare Beneficiary Program. This program is designed to pay your Medicare part B premiums. This program allows you to have a bit more income than the QMB program does. While the qualification rules vary by state, the basic rules are based on your income being 110 percent or less of the current "guideline figures." The guideline figures are what the Social Security Administration considers poverty level, currently roughly $10,000 for a family of two. Every January, these numbers change so you should call the SSA to ask for the most current poverty guidelines that pertain to the Specified Low Income Medicare Beneficiary Program.

MEDICARE PART B: MEDICAL INSURANCE	
BASIC COVERAGE:	80% of approved amounts exceeding the annual deductible of $100 Laboratory services: 100% of approved amounts for blood tests, biopsies
YOUR COSTS:	$100 each year plus 20% of approved amounts plus additional amounts charged by doctors who do not accept assignment
Home Health Care	100% of approved amounts for Medicare-approved services (no deductible) 80% of approved amounts for durable equipment (after deductible)
Medical - Outpatient Hospital Care	80% of approved amounts (after deductible)
Medical - Blood	80% of approved amount (after deductible) 20% of approved amount 20% of approved amount First 3 pints plus 20% of approved amount for additional pints (2)

SERVICE MEDICARE BENEFITS - YOUR COSTS
(Hospitalization)
$716 per benefit period in 1995
Full cost after deductible is met (1st - 60th day)
$179 per day co-insurance in 1995
Full cost after co-insurance (61st - 90th day)
Full cost after co-insurance for 60 life-time reserve days, or $0 after 60 reserve days are used.
$358 per day co-insurance in 1995
Full cost
Post-hospital care in a certified skilled nursing facility (SNF)
Intermediate and custodial nursing care
Home health care
Hospice
Blood
100% of approved amounts for $0 the first 20 days of care each benefit period after 3-day hospital stay
Full cost after co-insurance (21st - 100th day)
100% of approved amount of Medicare-approved services
80% of approved amount for durable medical equipment
$89.50 per day co-insurance in 1995
Full cost
Full cost
20% of approved amount in 1995
All but limited costs for outpatients drugs and inpatient respite care
Limited cost-sharing for outpatient drugs and inpatient respite care
Full cost after first 3 pints
First three pints

In addition to the income qualifications, if your assets are over a certain amount, you will not qualify for this program. The amounts are determined by the states and are tied to poverty limits. If you think you qualify for this program, contact your local Social Security office and request an application.

For specific guidelines in your state, visit the local Social Security/Medicare office or call one of the hotline numbers in the resource section of this text.

Religious organizations

These may be alternatives to help you cut costs. Many religious organizations have subsidized housing, aid and other ways to ease your burden.

MEDICARE PART B:
MEDICAL INSURANCE

Service	Medicare Benefits	Your Cost
Physician and surgical services, medical supplies, diagnostic tests, durable medical equipment	80% of approved amounts exceeding the annual deductible of $100	$100 each year plus 20% of approved amounts plus additional amounts charged by doctors who do not accept assignment
Laboratory services: Blood tests, biopsies, etc.	100% of approved amounts	$0
Home health care	100% of approved amounts for Medicare-approved services (no deductible)	$0
	80% of approved amount for durable medical equipment (after deductible)	20% of approved amount
Outpatient hospital care	80% of approved amount (after deductible)	20% of approved amount
Blood	80% of approved amount after first 3 pints	First 3 pints plus 20% of approved amount for additional pints (2)

Pharmaceutical programs

You may be entitled to free pharmaceuticals. Many prescription drug companies offer some of their products at no charge to older patients who cannot afford them. Contact your local congressional representative or the elder-care hotline numbers to ask for a list of each company's senior programs and eligibility requirements. Another useful bulletin you can get is "Programs to Help Older Americans Obtain Their Medications: An Information Paper Prepared by the Staff of the Special Committee on Aging," United States Senate (1994), available from a local Area Agency on Aging.

Convert your home

Convert your current home into a safe and more suitable residence for later life. Tricks for getting your home ready for your later years include:

- Improve lighting where shadows might make you miss a step.
- Have furniture that is easy to get in and out of.
- Acquire a reaching tool to get hard-to-reach items in the kitchen.
- Have a small ladder in your home. Keep heavy objects on shelves not too low and not too high.
- Avoid loose slippers that could get caught and cause you to trip.
- Place handrails on stairs and put nonslip material on the steps.
- In the bathroom, put nonslip material in the shower and tub. Anchor your bathroom rugs with two sided tape to avoid slippage. Also, install more grab bars around the tub and toilet area.

Home health care (HHC)

Some people say they will never set foot in a nursing facility. Unfortunately, you don't usually have a choice. If you're suddenly debilitated by a stroke or Alzheimer's, you're not aware of what is happening. Other people may have to choose home health care for you or another loved one.

Home health care has been growing in popularity. As you read in the Medicare section of this text, Medicare is under cost-containment and fewer home care services are being provided for by Medicare. Medicare does not cover nonmedical services. Unfortunately, many costs related to home health care are nonmedical in nature. As a result, senior citizens paid more than two billion dollars out of their savings to pay for these costs last year. Non-medical costs usually mean personal assistance, such as help getting out of bed. Surveys show that there is a high percentage of people living at home who cannot perform one or two of five activities of daily living, and there's an even higher percentage of people living at home who cannot perform three or more ADL. There are actually more people living at home that cannot perform one or more ADL than people in nursing homes. It makes sense for someone recovering from an operation or an illness not serious enough to require constant professional medical care to stay at home. If a spouse or other loved one is available to act as a caregiver, home health care is an ideal alternative to long-term care.

It is extremely important to remember that HHC is not free. Professionals come to your home on a regular basis to perform a service. In addition, equipment may have to be rented and supplies will have to be bought. However, studies show that, on average, HHC is less expensive than LTC.

In certain cases, Medicare will pay on a limited basis for in-home respite care for a chronically dependent individual. The maximum time covered is 35 hours of care per week. However, as with other Medicare programs, there are many rules governing this coverage. If you fail to meet one of the criteria, you will lose the Medicare benefit.

Typically, it is Medicare part A that will pay for home health care services if you qualify. The qualification requirements include:

1. You must be homebound.

2. You must be under a physician's care and have a specific treatment plan signed by your doctor.

3. You must only need part-time or intermittent home health services requiring skilled service.

4. The care must be provided by an agency certified by Medicare.

Getting the fair amount that Medicare should pay

As stated above, to receive Medicare benefits, you must be in need of skilled services on an intermittent basis. The broad definition of skilled services usually includes tasks such as administering medication and changing catheters. Skilled care could include therapists who help stroke victims learn how to walk or talk. Services such as housecleaning and cooking are usually not covered. Intermittent tasks are usually defined as less than five days of care per week. The care can be as infrequent as once every 60 to 90 days.

Typically, Medicare will not pay for more than 35 hours a week of home health care. However, if you have a finite problem for a predictable period of time, usually no more than 21 days, you can get up to 56 hours a week of covered services. An example is if you have a specific injury that needs to heal for this time period.

The problem with Medicare is that once you reach a plateau—you are not getting any better, but your condition is stabilized—Medicare will likely discontinue service. (This is true even though everyone from your physician to your therapist knows that without continuing care, there is a high probability you will have a relapse or another illness.) Then, when you are well again, Medicare will resume coverage.

As explained in the long-term care insurance section of this book, in certain instances, a long-term care insurance policy will pay home health care. You can also buy a separate home health care insurance policy to pay for only home health care costs. However, you have to review these policies carefully because the coverage is often inadequate for home health care.

Studies have shown that people with chronic disabilities require an average of four to five home care visits per week for five to 10 years!

Check with agencies in your region including the Area Agency on Aging and Medicaid offices to see if any home health care services are available in your area.

Other alternatives to long-term care

There is no question that long-term care, whether it is in the home or in a care facility, is expensive. Certain organizations and services are available to help reduce the costs.

Homemaker services

Homemaker services are not covered under Medicare. These services usually include help in an activity of daily living such as food shopping, grooming or dressing.

The cost for these services runs from $10 to $20 per hour. Certain Medicare supplement policies and HMO plans cover these fees so you should ask if the services are covered when you're signing up for a Medicare supplement or HMO plan.

To find out about a homemaker service near you, call Eldercare Locato or contact the Area Agency on Aging in your community. (See Appendix 3.)

Home chore services and home maintenance/repair programs

These services help with domestic chores such as minor household repairs, cleaning, yard work, etc. The costs vary from $5 to $10 per hour, depending on where you live. Sometimes you can pay one low annual fee and receive help in case of an emergency, such as a pipe burst. To find a service in your community, contact an elder-care group.

Meals on Wheels/home-delivered meals

An alarming number of the elderly suffer from malnutrition because they either cannot shop or can't prepare meals on their own. These services are inexpensive and quite helpful.

Home sharing

Also increasing in popularity is the concept of home sharing, in which you share your house with someone else or you move into someone else's home. The benefit is that you share the maintenance expenses and nursing costs and also have companionship and the security of someone nearby if you need help.

There are home-matching programs to help people arrange house shares. One good resource is a nonprofit group:

Shared Housing Resource Center
6344 Greene St.
Philadelphia, PA 19144

Senior discounts

Millions of dollars are spent by American businesses trying to attract mature Americans as clients. Mature Americans comprise an unusually large percentage of the population and one that continues to grow. Also, mature Americans are exceptionally loyal to the products and services they use. As a result, companies offer many programs to attract this market segment. There are a wide range of discounts available including everything from reduced airline fares to low-cost rounds of golf to promotional rates for meals and entertainment. Don't assume these discounts are not worth your time. If you're a careful consumer, you can save thousands of dollars each year. You could put the money you save toward paying for long-term care insurance, save it for unexpected medical bills or perhaps help the less fortunate.

To get many of the discounts, you have to spend some time and effort. If there are two comparable services and one offers a special reduced rate simply because of your age, there's no reason not to take it. However, these savings are often not widely promoted. Even if you are entitled to the discount, you may have to ask whether it is available in order to receive it. The following list covers discounts available in most communities.

Popular senior discounts
1. Many financial institutions, such as banks, mutual fund companies and brokerage firms, will waive certain account fees. You may be eligible for no-fee checking accounts, free unlimited checks, etc.

2. You should always ask for travel and entertainment discounts. Most golf courses and tennis courts offer senior discounts. Call the local municipal parks, courts and courses. Sometimes these facilities offer free play or use during off-peak hours or charge seniors only a nominal fee.

3. Many national parks offer senior discounts.

4. Airlines usually permit older Americans to purchase a coupon book of deeply discounted tickets.

5. Most theaters, movie houses, operas and symphonies offer excellent discounts for seniors. Sometimes you can get discounts on individual tickets and other times you have to buy season tickets.

6. Hotels and travel clubs also offer excellent reduced-rate fares.

7. If you pay an annual fee for your credit card, ask if the company will waive its fee for you. Usually, if you have a good credit record and you ask, you'll receive this no-fee offer.

8. Discounts for many day-to-day purchases are often available if you ask ahead of time. For example, restaurants, department stores and grocery stores often have one day or selected hours when a senior discount is available.

9. Discounts on your "fixed expenses" are sometimes available, as well. Contact your local phone company, utility firm, water supplier or other service provider for information. These discounts can be set by your age, income or both.

It is silly to pay full price simply because you haven't asked whether a senior discount is available. Remember, though, that there are some unscrupulous people out there. Fraud is extremely prevalent in our society, especially among firms dealing with the elderly. You should exercise common sense. Work only with established reputable firms, regardless of how attractive an offer seems to be. Don't make purchases over the phone unless you're familiar with the company or are comfortable with the organization you're dealing with. Don't assume that something in a letter or in the newspaper is always true. If you're uncomfortable with an offer or item, do some research. Go to your local library and see if you can read back newspaper articles about the company. Call your local Better Business Bureau. Be skeptical if there is a post office box listed as the permanent address. Remember, if it sounds too good to be true, it probably is.

Summary

Too many people mistakenly assume that the government will somehow cover their nursing home stays. Unfortunately, the applicable government program—Medicare—covers only a small number of nursing home stays. You must be admitted to a facility after you have spent three days in a hospital and the facility must be Medicare approved. Even if you meet these qualifications, it's unlikely that Medicare will cover all of your costs. You will probably need to buy a Medicare supplementary policy to cover the costs that aren't covered by Medicare. Also, if you recover and return to your own home, you should investigate other private and public programs that can help you. These programs include Meals on Wheels, homemaker services, home repair services, etc.

Chapter 10

Overview of Medicaid

The following chart shows the minimum and maximum income levels used to determine your Medicaid eligibility.

MEDICAID ESTIMATED 1995 FIGURES	
Community Spouse Minimum Resource Standard	$14,532.00
Community Spouse Maximum Resource Standard	$74,820.00
Community Spouse Minimum Maintenance Standard	$1,178.75
Community Spouse Maximum Maintenance Standard	$1,816.50

Introduction

Recently, a widowed woman was sick and needed care in a nursing home. She gave her son power of attorney to manage her affairs. This woman's estate consisted of a home worth about $80,000 and a savings account with $15,000 in it.

The goal was to admit the woman into a nursing home as a private paying resident and then subsequently divest her of assets in order to have Medicaid cover the cost of the nursing home. To accomplish this, the son transferred to himself $1,000, his mother's home and the savings account. After nine months in the nursing home as a private payer, the son applied for Medicaid on his mother's behalf. The application included a question about whether any gifts were made within the past two years. The son forgot to mention the gift (it was a gift because the property was not transferred for fair market value). Medicaid found out that gifts were made and the Medicaid application was denied. Because she had no assets in her name, the mother faced discharge from the nursing home due to non-payment.

Unfortunately, this is a typical case. Most people simply don't plan ahead, or don't seek expert advice. Read on for a brief overview of the Medicaid system and some advice on plans you should make in order to use Medicaid. Bear in mind, though, that you should use this advice to provide general guidance. With regulations being updated and court rulings being made about Medicaid, it's important that you consult a specialist if you have a particular problem.

Medicaid is not Medicare. As you may know, most people age 65 or older, regardless of their financial situation, will receive Medicare benefits. Medicaid is a public benefit program supported by federal and state taxes designed to pay for certain medical costs when an individual does not have the financial resources to pay these costs. Most states and counties adapt the Medicaid program to fit the needs in that state or region. In some instances, the state even adopts a specific name; in California the system is know as Medi-Cal.

Nursing home costs range from an average of nearly $40,000 per year up to $100,000. How many people do you know who can afford $50,000 per year for long-term care for a sick spouse, and still maintain the standard of living for the well spouse? Probably not many. Medicaid pays for about half the people in nursing homes today. That would be fine except that *most people on Medicaid are broke.* The unfortunate truth is that most people entering nursing homes will spend every cent of their money within one year! You will have to spend most of your money before you receive any aid whatsoever from Medicaid.

It doesn't seem right that in order to receive Medicaid, you have to be penniless. After all, you have paid into Social Security and Medicare for many years, so you should be able to receive benefits if you have an illness requiring a nursing home stay. Our system works well when you have a tangible illness. When you break an arm or develop a cancer, you will probably receive some type of aid or entitlement. Yet, if you have a debilitating illness such as Alzheimer's or you have a stroke, you are required to spend-down all of your assets before being able to apply for Medicaid benefits.

Should you plan on receiving Medicaid benefits? You will have to make this decision when you work on your "elder-care plan." Plan to self-insure and hope that you will be eligible for some Medicaid payments, but you must plan ahead! Don't wait until you need the coverage, when it will be too late. Most people do not want to qualify for Medicaid because they may feel as if they are on welfare and don't want to accept this. Also, some elder-care specialists say that you receive a different level of care as a private patient compared to a Medicaid patient. Whether or not this is true, you must consider the consequences of being faced with an extraordinarily high medical bill for your care. If you are wealthy, chances are you can afford these medical costs. If you are poverty-stricken, you are almost assured care. The vast majority of the middle class have enough money saved for "normal" expenses, but not for long-term care. Everything you and your family worked for could be gone in only 12 months.

Before figuring out how to protect your assets, you should have a detailed knowledge of the Medicaid system. Remember, this chapter is meant to provide a simple overview. Any specific questions you have should be directed to Medicaid or an elder-care attorney in your area. Every state and most counties have different rules pertaining to Medicaid. You should understand these rules and how your state interprets the federal laws.

What is Medicaid?

Medicaid is a federal- and state-funded health insurance program for people who need financial aid for medical purposes. Although the requirements and program names vary from state to state, they are still part of the Medicaid system. If, for example, you were in a Medicaid-approved facility, and you "qualified" for Medicaid, certain expenses for medical care would be paid.

How to qualify for Medicaid—income and asset tests

This is the tricky part. Technically, in order to qualify for Medicaid, individuals must be impoverished. In 1989 the Spousal Impoverishment Act was passed. This Federal act set the guidelines that limit the total income and assets of Medicaid recipients in care facilities as well as the assets and income of their spouses. This act allowed for spouses of Medicaid recipients to retain or exempt certain assets in Medicaid's determination of your eligibility.

The act set forth a range of assets; each state has subsequently set the amounts in that range for their guidelines. Therefore, the state amount guidelines differ, but the two factors determining qualification—*household income* and *assets*—are used in all states.

How do I find out if my state is an income cap or benefit state?

There are two types of states—*income cap* and *benefit* (also known as "medically needy"). More and more states are turning to income cap, which means that you cannot receive Medicaid if your income is over the set limit. A benefit state follows the same guidelines with one major exception: If your income exceeds the limit, but is less than the average cost of nursing homes in your area, you may still be eligible for Medicaid. Also, in medically needy states, you can "spend-down" your money for medical needs. To the extent you do this, you can reduce your available income to bring you closer to allowable limits for Medicaid.

To find out if your state is an income cap or a benefit state, you should contact your local Area Agency on Aging, Social Security office, Welfare office or elder-care attorney (see Appendix 3).

Income test—first test

In 1994, the majority of states capped the well spouse's income limit for Medicaid eligibility at $1,266 per month, although some states allow as much as $1,720 per month. This amount is indexed to inflation and will increase slightly each year.

For single individuals, the income allowed for the Medicaid beneficiary is almost nil—just enough for a few incidentals.

Remember, if you live in a benefit state, you can usually petition to be allowed income over the set limit for certain reasons, such as if your rent or other fixed expenses are higher than the average in your community or if you have excessive long-term care expenses.

Strategies to keep your income low in order to qualify for Medicaid

If you plan ahead, you may be able to get your income low enough, and keep it low enough, to qualify for Medicaid.

Here are some ways to keep your income level low:

1. Take Social Security at 62 years of age to get the lower amount.

2. When you retire, take a lump sum instead of an annual guaranteed income.

3. Use investment options that let you control the stream of income or select investments that do not produce any income.

4. Move to a benefit state where the cost of nursing home care is greater than your income.

5. Consider putting your money into trusts.

6. If your caregivers are family members who are not paid, start paying them. If your caregivers are charging you fair wages for the services they are providing, such as running errands or paying your bills, then this money should not be considered a gift.

7. Petition Medicaid to request more income than the "monthly maintenance allowance" or "spousal allowance." Often you can show that the monthly maintenance allowance is insufficient to maintain your home and meet your basic needs. However, most of the income cap states will not permit you to have more than the state limits.

8. Many individuals try to transfer as many income sources as possible to the well spouse's name. This works best in Medical benefit states where there is no income cap. Even if the well spouse receives income over the Medicaid eligibility limit, the well spouse is allowed to receive an unlimited amount of income paid to him or her. All that the spouse will forfeit is his or her Community Spousal Resource Allowance (CSRA). For example, if the well spouse had no income but the sick spouse had $2,000 in income, the well spouse could still keep roughly $1,800 and still be able to qualify for Medicaid. If you assume the well spouse has income of $3,000 and the sick spouse wishes to go on Medicaid, if the sick spouse has no income, the well spouse should keep the full $3,000.

Asset test—second test

The second test you must pass to qualify for Medicaid eligibility purposes is the asset test.

The Spousal Impoverishment Act that went into effect in 1989 changed almost all the guidelines. The numbers vary from state to state, but married couples can maintain a certain amount of assets. You are allowed certain "exempt" assets and a specific amount of "nonexempt" assets.

The nonexempt assets that are allowed to be kept by the well spouse are known as the Community Spousal Resource Allowance (CSRA). The minimum nonexempt assets allowed are roughly $14,532 in most states, with a maximum of $72,600 (based on 1994 numbers). These amounts increase each year. Still, without proper planning, the most you could have in nonexempt assets is $72,600 (in 1994). Although the regulations vary, a good rule of thumb to figure out how much you can have is to take all of your nonexempt assets (cash stocks, real estate, bank accounts, etc.) and divide the assets by two. This number, or the maximum of $72,600, is what you could keep. If you have assets of $100,000, you can keep $50,000. This rule provides a good estimate, but often you can keep more than half of your estate.

What this means is that if the well spouse has more than $72,600 in assets, neither spouse will be eligible for Medicaid. However, the creative person who plans ahead and converts the assets over $72,600 into exempt assets can avoid this dilemma.

Exempt assets

An exempt asset is one that Medicaid does not include in the amount of assets allowed. You can keep these assets when you apply for Medicaid and while you receive Medicaid payments. Examples of exempt assets include:

1. **Your personal residence.** A married couple owning a home will not have to include their residence in the Medicaid asset limitations. Most states do not stipulate the size of the home or dollar value. However, usually one spouse must still be living in the house if it is used as an exempt asset. In addition, home furnishings, home improvements and collectibles are usually exempt assets.

    However, The Omnibus Reconciliation Act Amendment of 1983 tightened the rules. Although your home is protected during your lifetime, the federal government is encouraging states to lien homes after your death in order to recoup expenses.

2. **One car.** A car, of any dollar value, is exempt, so if you have an old car that is going to break down, you should think about buying a new one.

3. **Certain jewelry.** Usually a wedding or engagement ring.

4. **$1,500 cash value of a permanent insurance policy.** There are no limitations on how much term insurance you can have.

5. **Burial plot.** $1,500 maximum value.

6. **Certain irrevocable trusts.** If structured correctly in an appropriate trust, the principal could be exempt. A simple rule of thumb is that if you don't have access to or control of the money, then Medicaid should not be able to access your money either. Most trusts would have to be set up prior to applying for Medicaid and the duties of the trustee must already be predetermined and cannot change.

When establishing trusts, you must consult an attorney who keeps up with the rapidly changing state laws and rulings. Also, bear in mind that some trusts must comply with a more stringent "five year look-back" rule (see Chapter 11).

7. **Assets given away in the proper time frame.** If you give away assets in the proper time frame, Medicaid cannot come and re-capture the assets.

8. **Properly structured annuities and/or private pension plans.** In the past, annuities have been widely accepted planning tools for protecting assets. OBRA 93 left many ambiguous and vague areas in Medicaid planning. Elder-care attorneys and other interested parties have asked the Health Care Financing Administration for interpretations and opinions. However, it is likely to be a while before there is final determination of what this ruling means. For now, you should consult an attorney if you're using annuities or other pension plans to protect your assets. But be aware that these plans may not be protected in the future.

Now that you know what assets are generally protected, you must learn how to use these exemptions to your benefit. The following are strategies you can employ to protect your assets:

Strategies to help reduce your exposure to nonexempt assets

1. **Give away your money three years before applying for Medi-caid if you are worried that you may one day need nursing services.** Instead of staggering out the gifts, however, consider making a one-time gift. The longer you drag it out, the later the look-back period begins. Always assume the look-back period is three years. If you gave away $1,000,000 three years ago plus one day, Medicaid cannot ask for information about this money.

   If you are worried about giving outright gifts for some reason (such as giving them to a minor who may be irresponsible), make the gift into a special entity such as a trust. Be careful, though, if you have access to the funds, because there is a good chance that Medicaid can deem the proceeds available to you and assume you could use the funds to pay your care. If you do use a trust, get help structuring it properly so the transaction does not haunt you later.

Special tip: Although it is true that a great deal of creative planning can help protect assets from Medicaid, it is not always foolproof and it could cost you a great deal in legal fees and still be very restrictive. For those who plan ahead, consider a strategy of buying four years or so of long-term care insurance/home health care (or a combination), use the insurance and give away your assets before the three-year look-back rule takes affect. Once you are in a care facility (assuming the facility is Medicare/Medicaid certified) and after you run out of money, you are still entitled to remain in that same care facility as a Medicaid recipient (as long as you qualify).

2. **Pay off your home if you still have a mortgage on it.** Having money outside of your house would reduce your eligibility. If you pay off your house, the house is protected. Or you may consider buying a larger house. Remember, regardless of the size of your house, it is a protected asset.

   If you make home improvements or buy new furnishings or jewelry (within limitations), these assets would also be exempt from Medicaid. However, be aware that liens could be put on your property by the state after your death.

3. **Buy a new car.** If you are allowed one car, make sure you have a valuable new car that can also be used for medical purposes.

4. **Pay off debt.**

5. **If your income is too high and you live in a benefit state, petition Medicaid and ask for a higher income allowance.** Of course, you will have to prove that you need the extra income or you will suffer undue hardship.

   If you live in an income cap state, take full advantage of all the techniques available to keep your income low.

6. **Transfer ownership of your insurance policies.** Even if there is no immediate Medicaid threat, there are valid reasons why you should not own the life insurance policies when you are insured. In a life insurance policy, there are usually three entities—the insured (the person who is likely to die), the owner (usually the insured person) and the beneficiary (the person who is entitled to the insurance when the insured dies). Why does the insured need to be the owner? By being the owner, you increase your net worth. The cash value and, in certain cases, the death benefit is part of your gross estate value. This is money that Medicaid could take.

   Instead of being the owner, you should consider making someone else, perhaps a child or a trust, the owner. Some caveats are in order, however: By making someone else the owner, that person should pay the premium. You should consider gifting that person the money to pay the premium. But if you die within two years after you transfer an existing policy, the transfer may be included in your estate value. There are other rules, so you should talk to an expert if you're considering this strategy.

7. **Make sure your caregivers are being paid appropriately.** Have you ever thought about how much work your caregiver does for you? Assume your child helps pay your bills, does errands, acts as an advisor, etc. You should be paying that child, and it's important to set a precedent that you pay your caregivers well before you even think about applying for Medicaid. You may even be able to continue making this payment after you apply for Medicaid. Because a caregiver does something of value, you could argue that the payment is for these services and is not a gift. A problem often arises because family members refuse to take payment, but then try to get paid only after the relative has applied for Medicaid. Then, Medicaid often denies the payment saying it is an attempt to defraud Medicaid.

8. **Protect your liquid cash and investments.** If annuities are still viable planning options in your state consider using them. These planning tools go by different names, including private pension plans, private annuities, personal annuities, tax-deferred savings plans, etc.

9. **Utilize the proper trusts for your situation, in the proper time frame to protect your assets.**

Annuities for Medicaid planning

How might an annuity protect my assets?

Historically, annuities have worked as follows: You put in a sum of money. Then, at a future date, the annuity would "annuitize" and pay you a guaranteed income for a set number of years or for the rest of your life. While the income was guaranteed, you no longer had access to your principal. Many pension plans worked in the same way: You could choose to take either a lump sum or receive the guaranteed income.

With annuities offered through insurance companies, you could not choose how your money would be invested. However, as consumers became savvier investors and more knowledgeable about annuities, the insurance industry responded by developing products that allowed you greater control over your assets. A properly structured annuity, created for your benefit, has certain intrinsic advantages, including:

1. All assets in the annuity accumulate on a tax-deferred basis. If you frequently switch in and out of funds and pay capital gains tax, this is a key advantage. It is also advantageous if you own bonds or bond funds but do not need the income.

2. The income accumulated in your annuity is not included in your gross income and at the end of the year; it will not be included in your 1099 income statement. This is very important if you want your income to fall below the limits so you will not have to pay taxes on your Social Security. Remember, though, that while municipal bond interest is tax-free, it is still included in your gross income for Social Security purposes.

3. You do not have to give up access to your income or principal while you are healthy.

4. You can create these annuities in ways that let you choose where you want to direct the investments. You can select mutual funds, government bond funds, money market accounts (not insured by the FDIC), etc.

5. You may be able to use the annuity to create an exempt asset for Medicaid purposes. Thus, you could keep your money and still qualify for Medicaid. Check with an attorney or planner familiar with the laws in the state.

Simply creating an annuity and transferring your assets into it does not guarantee that the assets will be exempt—how the annuity is structured will determine this. You must follow certain rules and guidelines for exempting assets. If you use a prototype annuity, be sure the company issuing the contract allows you to put in the provisions as needed so that your assets are protected under the Medicaid guidelines.

Usually you can create the annuity and place both spouses' names on the contract, then name one of your children as the beneficiary. Assume you create this annuity and choose mutual funds in which to invest inside the annuity. You invest as you would normally—switching funds, taking income or reinvesting. If one spouse dies, the funds will not go through probate. The surviving spouse can keep the account active or liquidate and take the funds.

Note that once an annuity is created, it is very similar to an IRA. If you withdraw your funds prior to 59½ years of age you will have to pay 10 percent penalties, as well as tax on the money.

Assume you are planning to apply for Medicaid and one spouse gets sick. At this point, you would invoke the provisions that were established when you created your personal annuity.

The one transfer of assets that is allowed without disqualification under the three-year look-back rule is spousal transfer. Immediately make sure the annuity is in the healthy spouse's name. In addition, the beneficiary must not be the sick spouse. If the sick spouse is named as beneficiary, you will have to change the beneficiary to someone else or a separate trust.

If the annuity is transferred to the well spouse's name, you have accomplished two important steps. First, the money inside the annuity might be under the Community Spousal Resource Allowance (CSRA), and second, the annuity does not generate income that will help to keep your income below the Medicaid guidelines. This may be all the planning you need, depending on the size of your estate and your income.

Usually, your estate will still be worth more than the Medicaid allowance. You will now need to invoke certain provisions that were established when you originally created your annuity. You must begin a periodic payment stream of both principal and interest for a set number of years. You will have to figure out what the least amount of income and principal is that you can take in order to remain below the income limitations for Medicaid. Since you have created your own annuity, you can dictate any provisions you want. You could instruct the annuity to pay you, for example, nine dollars of interest per month and one dollar of principal. It's important you realize that you don't have to pay yourself all the income. Remember, you're using the annuity in order to keep your income below the Medicaid limits. This is a legitimate loophole in the Medicaid regulations.

Medicaid update warning

Creating a personal annuity to provide you with a stream of income and principal as described above has been used as a way to keep your income below Medicaid limits. However, recently, the Health Care Finance Administration (HCFA) has stated that if you use an annuity payout schedule that is not based on a mortality table, then the annuity would be considered a gift and subject to the look-back periods for Medicaid eligibility.

Therefore, you should get legal advice or check with Medicaid before establishing your annuity to make sure you comply with the latest requirements.

Some annuity companies will not pay whatever interest or principal you want. When you annuitize, many companies will base the payout on your age, the annuitant's age and how long you want to receive the income, along with mortality tables. Obviously the longer the payout, the lower the income will be—which is what you want if you're trying to protect your money. Even if you go for the longest payout option and get the lowest interest rate, many companies will allow you to change your mind (this is known as a Bail Out Provision), usually after five years. At this time, you could withdraw whatever is left in your account. It is the payout of the annuity that is usually the determining factor in whether you will qualify for Medicaid. In many income cap states, annuities provide no real advantage since a simple annuity payout will boost you up over the income cap, thereby disqualifying you for Medicaid.

The above strategy probably sounds like you "annuitized your annuity." For Medicaid purposes you did: The annuity is paying periodic payments of principal and interest, you don't have access to the principal (while you're on Medicaid) and the annuity has a set number of years for payments. However, you have also included provisions that allow for the income and principal payments to stop, say after five years, and the cash then becomes available and is paid to either the healthy spouse or the beneficiaries.

Remember, not all custodians allow you to break an annuity, so make sure the custodian you use to create your annuity knows that you intend to stop the annuity once you have annuitized.

Also, you may not want either you or your spouse to be named as the beneficiary. Medicaid might be able to make a claim on the asset if one spouse receives the money after the other spouse's death.

Furthermore, you might want to place someone else's name on the annuity as annuitant. You should do this well before the look-back period so that the annuity is not considered a gift.

There are several advantages to using someone else as annuitant. First, having someone other then yourself as annuitant, while you're still the owner, could be an excellent way to transfer the income to the annuitant. You may also be able to reduce the amount of income by combining your mortality with that of the annuitant. If the annuitant is younger than you, the income stream will be lower, once again helping to reduce your income for Medicaid eligibility purposes.

One very complex strategy that has been used is making your living trust the owner of your annuity. In doing so, the living trust has a provision stating that if you apply for Medicaid benefits, you are no longer trustee and lose access to the trust's assets. However, this strategy has been frowned on by Medicaid and you should only use it if you have consulted an attorney who feels your trust will comply with Medicaid guidelines.

How does my annuity fit in with my other investments?

Most annuities let you select from a wide range of options, including mutual funds and other investments that can have a range of low to high risk, depending on your choices.

What are the costs?

Maintaining an annuity does not have to cost a significant amount of money if you understand how the annuity works. As with other investments, you have to pay attention to a broker's commission and other loads you pay when you invest in mutual funds.

Setting up an annuity requires you to consult with an attorney or financial planner. As with any expert you consult, ask for references and find out what education or professional degrees the expert has. Check with at least two experts to make sure that you're not paying excessive fees to establish the annuity.

Caution!

Annuities are not appropriate for everyone. Make sure you're comfortable with the insurer managing the annuity. Look for reputable companies that are not likely to go out of business. Also, remember that while an annuity might permit you to maintain your income under Medicaid regulations today, these regulations can change. You should check with an attorney to make sure your annuity complies with the regulations.

Trusts for Medicaid planning

Using trusts can be incredibly tricky and confusing. However, there are viable trusts that can be utilized in certain circumstances. Again, it's important to check with a specialist who is familiar with the laws in your community before you set up a trust for Medicaid planning purposes.

All trusts operate in the same basic way: The person who creates the trust is known as the *trustor, creator, settlor* or *grantor*. The person in charge of the trust who is empowered to make decisions is the *trustee*. A *successor trustee* is the person next in line, should something happen to the existing trustee. The recipient of the trust, the person who will receive the trust proceeds, is the *beneficiary*. A valid trust must have something in it, such as cash, real estate, securities, etc. These assets are the *corpus* or *principal*.

In some cases, the beneficiary is actually the trustor. You establish a trust for a period of time in order to get assets out of your name and control. You name a trustee to manage the assets and at a later date, you would get back the assets. This was the aim of the Medicaid qualifying trust that is no longer a viable option as a result of OBRA 93. However, the rules are still being questioned in court and opinion about what trusts are valid varies, even among elder-care attorneys. You might get one opinion from one lawyer while another will provide the opposite advice. Some attorneys have asked for clarification by the Health Care Finance Administration, and some court decisions have gone against the lower rulings.

Because of the many changes and the lack of court precedents, you cannot rely on one technique as a guaranteed way to protect your assets. Consult an experienced elder-care specialist for guidance and make any decisions about trusts quite carefully. Even with the best advice, you may find that at some point in the future, the government may deem your strategy inappropriate.

The following are a few examples of trusts that people have used under various circumstances to help shelter assets in order to apply for Medicaid.

Miscellaneous trusts

It's worth stressing again that using trusts is a risky proposition with regard to Medicaid. It's unlikely that you want to be a test case, so you should consider any of these options as possibilities, but not guaranteed ways to protect your assets.

Trigger trusts operate as follows: You state in advance when income would be paid to the Medicaid beneficiary and when it would be stopped, timed to the 36-month look-back rule.

Income only trusts were popular at one time. You put all your assets in the trust and the trust could only pay out income. These trusts don't work in an income-cap state where the income will probably be over the Medicaid limit and result in the person being disqualified for Medicaid.

Irrevocable trusts that don't give you discretion or access to the assets, or the right to change the trusts, seem to be allowed under the new regulations, as long as the trust was established prior to the look-back period. But you should realize that these trusts are like giving a gift to someone—the asset is not yours. The only reason to create the trust is to have stipulations on the gift. Say you want to give $1,000,000 to a child three years before you enter a nursing home, but you're nervous about giving such a large gift to a child. You could establish this type of trust and comply with a five-year look-back period. However, you should be aware that a *revocable trust* that gives the trustor full discretion over the assets is not an effective way to protect your assets from Medicaid.

It's worth stressing again that even if you have a *Medicaid Qualifying Trust* that had been established to protect your assets from Medicaid, it is no longer valid as a way to protect your assets. Under OBRA 93, these trusts were not grandfathered and given protection. If an adviser suggests that you use one of these trusts, tell the adviser that these trusts are no longer valid.

Special or Supplemental Needs Trusts/Support Trusts

Prior to OBRA 93 many types of trusts, especially Special Needs Trusts and Support Trusts were used. A Special Needs Trust was designed to give the beneficiary of the trust, usually the Medicaid recipient, benefits for some items, such as dental work, grooming, etc. These trusts are also a way to create a trust for a disabled child as a means to keep assets from the child or other person who did not want to be disqualified from any public benefits. Support Trusts are those trusts designed to support an individual and pay for their housing. OBRA regulations have made these trusts more restrictive.

Medicaid has stipulated how and which trusts can be used. But the interpretations are still developing and there is not much case law yet. Still, it seems easier to establish a Special Needs Trust rather than a Support Trust.

The OBRA 93 did outline three exceptions that allow specific trusts to work without disqualifying you for Medicaid eligibility. These are (d)-4A, (d)-4B and (d)-4C trusts.

OBRA (d)-4A Exception Trusts

If you use this trust creatively, it could be a viable planning tool. To create a (d)-4A trust these requirements must be met:

1. You must be under age 65.
2. You must be disabled according to the Social Security definition of disability.
3. The trust must be created by a child, parent, guardian or court.

You could literally create one of these trusts the day before applying for Medicaid. However, if you are over 65 you simply can not set up the trust. The disability definition is not as tough as you think. If someone is about to enter a nursing home, chances are that person is disabled or can be proven to be disabled to the court. Often, the parents are deceased so you will have to ask the court to create a trust for you or your children.

Once everyone agrees that the trust can be created, assets are funneled into it. The look-back period does not apply. However, maintaining the trust can still be confusing. It is not clear how the trustee can distribute assets or what is the standard of distribution. Some Medicaid experts feel the supplemental needs trust is too restrictive, but, on the other hand, with a true support trust, you will probably have too much income for Medicaid eligibility.

Probably, the trust would work as a discretionary trust. The trustee has the discretion to decide how and when assets are distributed. If too much money is distributed in any one month, you may lose public benefits for that month.

The catch to this trust is what happens after the Medicaid beneficiary dies. Your state will claim your trust in order to recapture all of the money they spent on your care. To avoid the state claiming your money, it would seem appropriate for the trustee to constructively spend the trust down to nothing.

In summary, be very careful when creating these trusts. Look at the state rules regarding limits to the amount of money in the trust and from what sources the money can come.

OBRA (d)-4B Exception Trusts (Miller Trusts)

This trust is designed for those who are domiciled in income cap states. These states have established an income cap on the amount that a well spouse in a community could receive and still be eligible for Medicaid.

You may have no assets but still have income. The concept behind this trust is that it is wrong to deny a person Medicaid if he or she has no assets but still has income exceeding the Medicaid limit. A case went to court over this issue (thus the name Miller Trust) and the court agreed that Medicaid applicants who have income in excess of the state income cap should qualify for benefits as long as certain criteria are met. The court ruled that the trust beneficiary—the Medicaid applicant—was incapacitated and in desperate need and the court had a duty to protect the incapacitated.

The first two criteria are relatively simple: First, the beneficiary of the income must be the Medicaid applicant. Second, all of the individual's income, including regular income, pensions, interest, etc., must be paid into the Miller Trust.

The next criteria are more complicated. The trustee is allowed to distribute a monthly income to the beneficiary, the Medicaid applicant, which is at least one dollar less than the state cap. This would allow the beneficiary to qualify for Medicaid under the income guidelines. The second rule states that after the Medicaid recipient dies, the remaining assets in the trust are to be paid to the state. But it is unclear whether the trust can give money to relatives or anyone else, such as family members who helped out. Also, it's not clear what happens to the excess income. Some states say it can't be used for any purposes even if you could use it to pay for supplemental needs.

OBRA (d)-4C Exception Trusts

This trust is much different from the (d)-4A and (d)-4B trusts. The general requirements for creating this trust are:

1. You can be any age.

2. You need to be disabled.

3. Assets have to be given to a "pooled income trust."

4. It must be established by parents, grandparents, guardian or a court.

Think of a pooled income trust as a mutual fund that is set up by a nonprofit agency as a "master trust." You put your assets into this pooled income fund, which is sponsored by a nonprofit agency. Your money is combined with that of other people and assets are purchased.

Medicaid allows this trust probably because the assets that are left over after a person dies go back into programs to help other people or to benefit Medicaid in some way.

Other advanced estate planning and asset-protection tools

People use estate planning vehicles for a myriad of reasons. Some people are trying to protect the estates from estate taxes. Others are trying to protect assets from lawsuits. And still others are working toward protecting their assets from nursing home spend-down. An estate planning tool commonly used for one purpose might be used for another, such as Medicaid planning. The following vehicles are advanced estate planning techniques not commonly used to protect assets but may be instrumental in this area. They will probably not work, however, unless they are established and implemented prior to the 36-month look-back rule.

Family limited partnership

Earlier in this chapter, you read about how you could go into a nursing home and either privately pay or use long-term care insurance for three years. Prior to the three years, you should give away your money. Instead of making an outright gift, why not consider creating a family partnership?

Typically a limited partnership would be created and assets would be gifted to this partnership. The owners of the limited partnership are generally the limited partners who are usually your children or grandchildren. The limited partners typically own 98 or 99 percent of all the shares. The general partners are usually the giver of the assets (the parents), and they keep only 1 to 2 percent of the actual ownership or shares in the partnership. The appealing aspect of the partnership is that the limited partners have no control, voting rights or any other rights. As limited partners, they own shares but have no say. Conversely, the general partner does not own the assets any longer but still maintains all voting rights.

Creating a family partnership can be very complicated, and there are some potential pitfalls. First, by giving away the assets while you are alive, you may trigger gift taxes and the assets tax basis will not step up upon the owners death. However, certain discounting techniques are often employed to help reduce the gift tax problem. Sometimes creators of family partnerships make the general partner a corporation, of which the parents are the officers. This is designed to insulate the general partner even further from lawsuits and creditor claims. Furthermore, if the general partner takes a "salary" for administering the partnership, the income could go directly into the corporation. This could potentially be a good technique for Medicaid planning, since there would be no income per se coming to the individuals and no asset ownership. For Medicaid planning purposes, you may want to go one step further and make a loved one or trusted adviser the general partner to remove yourself from all incidence of ownership. If a sick spouse gets better or dies, there could be some form of an income or special distribution that could be made later. This is a better option than making an outright gift.

Obviously, Medicaid is going to scrutinize this strategy and look for every reason to count this as an asset or source of income. However, if you establish the partnership properly, in the time-frame specific to Medicaid qualifications, a strong argument exists for further researching the creation of a family limited partnership.

Summary

Medicaid is a true bureaucracy. You have to work hard in order understand and utilize its services. First, learn how Medicaid works in your area. Talk with local agencies and find out which of your assets are exempt from inclusion in Medicaid's eligibility requirements. If you have too much income and too many assets, talk to a lawyer about utilizing legal strategies, such as trusts and annuities to protect your assets. Be cautious, though, because Medicaid has made it difficult to protect your assets. Trusts that enabled you to keep your assets just a few years ago no longer work. Seek help from a qualified elder-care lawyer to make certain you employ the right strategy, and be prepared for a long, hard fight in order to get your fair share.

Chapter 11

Additional considerations for Medicaid planning

The Omnibus Reconciliation Act of 1993 (OBRA 93)

The Omnibus Reconciliation Act that passed in August of 1993 dramatically changed the rules for Medicaid. There are three significant revisions.

1. Prior to OBRA 93, the look-back period regarding giving away assets was 30 months. OBRA extended this look-back period to three years for individuals and five years for trusts.

2. OBRA 93 clarified the definition of exempt assets as applied to Medicaid eligibility. However, the exempt assets are not exempt for estate recovery purposes. After someone dies, traditionally exempt assets, such as homes, are being liened by Medicaid to collect reimbursement for benefits that the agency provided to a recipient during his or her lifetime.

3. In fact, states are aggressively trying to recover and lien property, such as personal residences, that were considered exempt assets.

4. OBRA 93 specifically discussed certain trusts and their impact on a person's Medicaid eligibility. The regulation states that a Medicaid Qualifying Trust, which had been used in the past, would make the person ineligible for Medicaid.

The look-back rule

Unfortunately, you can't give away all your assets the day before you apply for Medicaid. There are specific time periods in which you can give away money. This is what is known as the *look-back rule*. In the past, the time period in which you could give away money had been shorter. However, OBRA extended this period and made the rules stricter as well.

Transferring assets

The look-back or transfer rules attempt to discourage a person from "transferring" or giving away assets in order to become impoverished and therefore eligible for Medicaid.

Any gift transfer of resources, such as cash, securities, real estate, etc., by an applicant or his or her spouse during the 36-month period preceding an application renders that applicant ineligible for nursing-home benefits. If you transfer assets from a trust, the look-back period could be 60 months or five years. Before OBRA, the period ran from the date the applicant was institutionalized, as well as when he or she applied for Medicaid. If the applicant was not institutionalized when he or she applied, the look-back period ran back from the date of the Medicaid application.

Most gifts made during the three years before applying for Medicaid will result in a period of disqualification for benefits. However, Congress has retained three important additional rules that modify the impact of the extended look-back period:

1. The period of ineligibility still begins with the month of the transfer and, as a result, may be exhausted by the date of application for benefits.

2. Transfers of exempt assets do not trigger any period of ineligibility.

3. If all transferred assets are returned, the disqualification is canceled.

There is also a special and very ambiguous rule for certain events involving trusts. The rule states that the look-back period is 60 months "in the case of payments from a trust or portions of a trust that are treated as assets disposed of by the individual [to another person from a revocable trust established by the beneficiary or when a beneficiary settler is foreclosed from receiving any benefits from an irrevocable trust]." This language appears to require that payments made to third parties from a revocable trust established by the Medicaid applicant or spouse will be subject to the special 60-month rule. This rule doesn't make much sense because you could simply transfer assets out of the trust name and back into your individual name before divesting yourself of the assets. That would make you subject to the 36-month (three-year) look-back, not the 60 months (five years).

If I gift assets incorrectly, could I be ineligible for periods longer than three years?

Yes, in fact, the period of time could almost be unlimited. If you give a gift during the three-year look-back period, it could extend your period of ineligibility to Medicaid for many years. If you apply for Medicaid within 36 months of making a gift, you could get a longer look-back than 36 months or five years for a trust.

Under both the old and the new law, the period of ineligibility resulting from such gift transfers is determined by dividing the amount of the gift by the statewide average monthly cost of nursing-home care. This rule serves to eliminate the incentive to make the gift.

Under the old law the period of ineligibility resulting from a gift transfer was "capped" at 30 months. Therefore, the incremental value of a gift over about $90,000 incurred no additional period of ineligibility because a gift of $90,000 already caused the maximum 30-month disqualification period ($90,000 divided by about $3,000 per month for nursing home costs).

Under the new law, there may no longer be any monthly cap. A very large gift could theoretically cause a disqualification period of many years. In practice, of course, a well-advised prospective applicant would simply wait out the 36-month look-back period and then apply for Medicaid. The moral of the story: Don't apply for Medicaid for 36 months after giving the gift.

You can easily calculate the period of disqualification based upon the amount of money transferred to a third party. The rule is to take the amount that you transferred and divide it by 3,000. The result is the number of months that you will be disqualified from receiving Medicaid benefits.

For example, assume that you transferred $60,000 to your daughter. Divide 60,000 by 3,000 and the result equals 20. This means you will be disqualified from receiving benefits for a period of 20 months.

Let's try a second example. Assume a $300,000 home was transferred to your daughter and a period of 36 months had not elapsed. Divide 300,000 by 3,000. The result is *100 months or 8 1/3 years!*

If, on the other hand, you transferred the funds prior to the 36-month look-back rule, you would not have a period of ineligibility.

This graphically illustrates the extreme importance of considering *when* to apply for state benefits.

The longer look-back period affects more than nursing homes

Under the old law, if a transfer caused a period of ineligibility, it applied only to a nursing facility and similar institutional care services. The disqualification rules now extend beyond institutional care and include certain forms of noninstitutional long-term care—including but not limited to home health care services, community supported living arrangements and other medical care.

The new look-back rule affects a wide range of assets

Previously, the transfer rules covered "resources," but not certain forms of income. The new rules now more broadly cover transfers of "assets," and assets include both resources and income of both the applicant and his or her spouse. As a result, you can no longer transfer away income, such as a lump sum windfall, to avoid a period of disqualification. The only way around this rule may be to create a trust which is effective in limited situations.

In addition, assets now also include any assets the applicant could have received but did not because of his or her spouse's action or because of the action of an agent or other legal representative, such as a conservator.

Finally, assets include the assets of either spouse.

Other significant restrictions to the new law

1. **Joint tenancy.** The new rules provide that any assets held in joint tenancy or a "similar arrangement" will be treated as having been transferred if either the applicant or any other person takes any action that reduces or eliminates the individual's ownership or control. In other words, if a daughter withdraws money from a bank account held jointly with her mother, a disqualifying transfer seems likely to arise for the mother, even if the funds clearly belong to the daughter. This rule may be disputed because it is likely to trap more applicants than it was intended to.

2. **Multiple gifts.** Under the old law, each gift transfer set off its own period of ineligibility, and these periods could run concurrently. Medicaid eligibility could often be accelerated by breaking gifts into smaller pieces. The new law, however, calculates the period of ineligibility by adding up the "total, cumulative uncompensated value of all assets transferred" before dividing by the cost of care.

Also, the new rules provide that no disqualification periods run from the dates of transfers during other periods of disqualification.

3. **Gifts by spouses.** The transfer rules now clearly cover transfers by either the applicant or his or her spouse. Under the new rules, the states can use a reasonable methodology to allocate any period of ineligibility between the applicant and spouse if the spouse later requires medical care subject to ineligibility from transfers.

Are there any exceptions to the look-back law?

A few rare exceptions exist:

1. **Returned transfers.** A disqualification is not imposed if "all assets transferred for less than fair market value have been returned to the individual."

2. **Hardship waivers.** The old law theoretically allowed an applicant to be released from a period of ineligibility if the denial of eligibility would impose "an undue hardship." Congress has amplified the hardship provision to require new federal procedural standards and substantive criteria from the Department of Health and Human Services (HHS). However, you should be aware that it often takes years for federal regulations to be approved. Since states have rarely granted hardship exceptions in the past, it's unlikely that you'll receive protection from this provision.

3. **"Sole Benefit" transfers.** The new rules continue the exemption for transfers to the individual's spouse or to "another for the sole benefit of the individual's spouse." Also, the exemption is extended to include transfers from the individual's spouse to another for the sole benefit of the spouse. This language may allow you some planning opportunities. So far, though, no one knows what is needed to prove that the "sole benefit" requirement has been met.

4. **Transfers to trusts for the elderly and disabled children.** The new rules retain the exemption for transfers to a disabled child. They also create additional exemptions for transfers to a trust created solely for a disabled child or for a disabled adult under age 65. You should consider these transfer exceptions in view of the new rules on treatment of trusts.

What are the relevant dates regarding the new rules?

The new transfer provisions do not apply to:

1. Medical assistance provided for services furnished before October 1, 1993.

2. Assets "disposed of" (presumably "transferred") on or before the date of enactment, August 10, 1993.

Later-in-life marriages

It may be advisable for you to consider a later-in-life marriage or a re-marriage. Certain benefits, such as Spousal Social Security and disability benefits, apply only if you're married. Sometimes, pension benefits or insurance will be paid only to a spouse. There may be tax advantages if you're able to use both spouse's exemption allowances.

However, as far as Medicaid is concerned, once you are married, the assets are community assets. Medicaid doesn't care that the assets were yours prior to marriage or that you have a prenuptial agreement or that the assets are not in both of your names. Your assets could be wiped out rather quickly if you expect to need Medicaid in the future. You should consider marriage very carefully, weighing all these considerations. It may not sound romantic, but it's in your best interest to look at the consequences of tying the knot.

Is divorce an option?

You may have heard tragedies about couples who divorce in order to protect their assets from Medicaid. It's sad, but sometimes couples divorce to avoid going broke. Unfortunately, this tactic doesn't always work.

Assume Thelma and Harry have been married for 40 years. Harry develops Alzheimer's disease. Thelma figures the cost of care will exceed hundreds of thousands of dollars over the next few years. She would be bankrupt. To avoid this event, she files for divorce. Do you think a judge will award Thelma 100 percent of the estate? It's unlikely, because Harry is incapacitated and the judge does not know exactly what Harry wants.

Assume that this is a second marriage for Thelma and Harry and they each have children from prior marriages. The judge is unlikely to give everything to Thelma in this case as well.

If divorce is an option, consider the ramifications in advance and plan carefully.

1. Try to initiate the divorce before the sick spouse is incapacitated.

2. Have a good reason for divorce, other than to protect assets from Medicaid.

3. The sick spouse should transfer all the "nonexempt" assets into the well spouse's name and explain that one spouse wants the other to have all the assets if there is a divorce.

Even if you've used these guidelines, the judge still might not give all the assets to one spouse. Although divorce may be an option, it is not always a cure-all.

Summary

With the laws constantly changing, you should double-check any advice you're given. Try to understand the changes made in OBRA 93 on your own, but also discuss your own situation with a knowledgeable senior adviser. The law affects the look-back rule, gifting and joint tenancy holdings. Don't forget that a marriage or divorce will also affect your Medicaid planning. You should use the system when you need to, and if you have problems, challenge it. Remember, though, that one decision you make can affect other aspects of your financial life. Make your decisions carefully. Play chess instead of checkers—look at how your move now will affect not just the next move, but the next and the next.

Chapter 12

Medicaid planning for the unmarried (single or widowed)

Unfortunately, planning for a single person is even more difficult than planning for a couple. The primary reason is, married couples have the Community Spousal Resource Allowance. This is the allowance by Medicaid that gives the well spouse a certain amount of income and assets that are exempt from Medicaid. Other reasons it is difficult to plan for Medicaid for a single person include:

- You cannot take advantage of spousal transfers.

- Your home may have a lien placed on it after the Medicaid recipient passes on.

- The income and asset allowance for single people is almost nonexistent.

The reason a home is a protected asset is because one spouse (or tenant) is living in the home. However, if there is not another tenant in the home, the house would usually not be considered a protected asset.

To get around this problem, these popular tactics are often used:

1. **If your home is liened, fight the lien.** California liened several homes upon the deaths of surviving spouses to collect money that was spent on Medicaid benefits. A class action lawsuit was filed, charging the state with not following the proper channels for a lien process. The court ruled for the homeowners and their survivors. It's worth fighting, even on a technicality, if your home is liened.

2. **Give away your money three years before applying for Medicaid.** Medicaid has no business asking you what money you had or what you did with it, as long as it was transferred prior to the look-back period. You should try to be creative with how you give away the money. You should talk to an attorney about using estate planning tools, such as trusts for your personal residence that could permit you to continue living in the home without owning it; creating a charitable trust; or owning a trust in another country.

3. **Get a letter of intent.** You may be able to protect your home with a doctor's help. If you can get a doctor to sign a letter of intent, stating that your stay in a nursing home is temporary and that you should be able to move back to your home in a short period of time, usually six months, then your house would be protected.

4. **Create a life estate.** You, as a parent, sign the deed over to your children or other beneficiaries. As long as you are alive, the children have no rights or access to the home. When you apply for Medicaid, your home is protected, since, technically, it is not yours. Upon your death or the death of your spouse, the home would go to your children or other beneficiaries. Unfortunately, since the passage of OBRA, these life estates are not working as they once did in all states. Before employing this strategy, check with an attorney in your state to make certain this tactic will still protect your house. In addition, there may be tax consequences to this strategy.

5. **Employ trusts that are permitted under OBRA.** Using these trusts properly should still allow you to protect some assets. You should know, though, that courts could rule that a trust does not comply with the OBRA requirements, or after you or your spouse die, Medicaid could try to seize the assets in the trust.

6. **Utilize annuities.** Although the income limitation is very low for single individuals, a carefully structured annuity might work. By designating someone else as the annuitant, you are allowing that person to be the recipient of all the income, thus insuring that your income will not be increased. In addition, you may be able to lower the income by combining the mortality of you, as the owner, with that of the annuitant. However, because you are still the owner, this arrangement could be viewed by Medicaid as a gift and therefore subject to the look-back rules. To avoid this problem, you should consider creating an annuity and naming someone else as annuitant long before the look-back period.

You will also have to designate someone else as the beneficiary. If you are the beneficiary, when you die, Medicaid might have a claim to the assets. While you will lose control of the principal while you are on Medicaid for a set number of years, it is better to keep your money and lose some control than to use up all your hard-earned money to pay for health care. If you "annuitize" an annuity and do it prior to the 36-month look-back period, it's unlikely Medicaid would try to seize the asset.

Sometimes you cannot transfer the income. If this is the case, you should still consider naming another person, someone very young, as the annuitant. Many annuity contractual provisions allow you to combine the owner's mortality rate with the annuitant's to start an annuitization payout schedule of a very low amount. This will help to keep you below the income limitations of Medicaid. If courts interpret OBRA and rule that the payout must be based on the owner's mortality, then this strategy will not be effective and you would probably exceed the income limits and be disqualified for Medicaid.

Again, you must bear in mind the look-back rule, gift tax and other issues that apply to your situation.

7. **Consider a reverse mortgage.** You may be surprised to learn that you can own a home worth a great deal of money but otherwise have very little income or other assets. This strategy led to the creation of the reverse mortgage—a means of tapping into the equity in your home. When a home has a great deal of equity, with little or no mortgage outstanding, you may be able to give up some portion of the equity or future appreciation for a guaranteed income.

This strategy can be useful for two reasons. First, you would have more income to help you pay your day to day expenses, medical bills, etc. Unfortunately, you would have to make sure that income stays below the Medicaid limit.

Second, you can create a reverse mortgage so that you still own the property, (to avoid transfer restrictions) but establish an irrevocable very low income stream over many years. You may be able to make the income lower and last longer by having a combined owner who is much younger. By making the reverse mortgage irrevocable, you should be able to avoid a Medicaid lien after your death. This strategy is new and your state may already have imposed restrictions on it but it's worth considering. Consult an expert who is knowledgeable about the latest regulations and court rulings in this area in your community.

You must be especially careful of the mortgage companies you use when you take out a reverse mortgage. Since the plans are new, some mortgage companies have been offering terrible deals and some outright scams. Look out for hidden fees and charges and be very careful before signing a reverse mortgage commitment.

8. **Use advanced estate planning tools, such as family limited partnerships.** These could be viable planning techniques if devised for Medicaid purposes. Your ownership in the partnership should be minimal (one percent of the partnership). Your discretion to take income or distributions should be minimal. You may even consider naming another person or entity the general partner. By all means, create this document transferring the assets into the partnership prior to the 36-month look-back period, and have a Medicaid specialist review the validity for your particular situation and jurisdiction.

Summary

While Medicaid is designed to allow a spouse to keep a certain amount of assets, stricter rules apply to single individuals, widows or widowers. You will have a more difficult planning process if you're single. Still, you can utilize annuities, trusts, reverse mortgages or letters of intent from physicians to protect your assets. It's essential that you plan well ahead of time. It's usually too late to protect your assets if you have to enter a care facility immediately.

Chapter 13

The details of Medicaid

The Medicaid application is a long technical document that will require a great deal of time to fill out properly. You should contact an attorney or adviser specializing in this field or contact the Area Agency on Aging office for other agencies that can provide help in completing the application.

Prior to filling out the actual application, contact your nearest Medicaid office (see "Medicare carriers by state" in the appendix). Once you find the office, explain to the Medicaid counselor that you are considering applying for Medicaid, and that you would like a *Medicaid assessment*. An assessment is important because it will show you how Medicaid looks at your financial situation, how they are valuing your assets and how much income Medicaid lists for you. After meticulously reviewing your assessment, you should dispute whatever you think is inaccurate. For example, you may own a piece of real estate that has lost its value while Medicaid may list the property at its former higher value.

After you receive the assessment and check it for accuracy, you can begin submitting your Medicaid application. Also, you can fill out an application and dispute the findings of a Medicaid assessment as many times as you find necessary. Don't be afraid to fill out an application for Medicaid more than once.

Tips on surviving the Medicaid application process

1. When filling out the Medicaid application, don't include more information then is required.

2. Medicaid will ask for a list of documentation. Do not give any original documents. Hand deliver the information that is requested and let a Medicaid employee make photocopies. Always get the name and signature of a person taking your information.

3. Take detailed notes of every phone conversation and personal interview. If you turn over any documents during an interview, ask the interviewer to sign a receipt for the papers.

4. Assume you will need accurate information about all of your assets including banks statements and mortgage papers. Approval will be held up until Medicaid has the required documents. Therefore, you should order bank statements and other asset documentation even before you're asked for it.

Disputing a Medicaid decision

If you've been rejected for a certain benefit and you feel you are justified in receiving it, you should speak out. Sometimes there are clerical mistakes with your paperwork and other times you may not have been given proper instructions from Medicaid counselors.

After you go through the application process, you will receive written notice stating that you have either been approved or denied for Medicaid benefits. If your application has been denied, you are allowed to appeal the decision. Usually the first appeal is informal so you shouldn't hesitate making one.

The written statement notifying you of your Medicaid denial includes details about the appeals procedure. Usually you must respond or begin the appeal process within 60 days.

You should be well-prepared for the appeal. Before the hearing, find out what is in your file. Medicaid has to provide you access to the file so that you can see what your records contain. Make sure you have written documentation substantiating your argument. Ask that anyone who has firsthand knowledge of relevant information accompany you to the appeal hearing.

The outcome of your appeal will be given to you in writing, usually within 90 days. If you lose the appeal, you can again appeal the decision; this appeal must be made within 30 days. It may be that you weren't prepared or didn't have the necessary documents. On occasion, the Medicaid referee makes an error. Don't be intimidated by the procedure—if you're fairly certain that you're entitled to Medicaid benefits, you should appeal and ask for a re-hearing at the same level.

In certain states you can request a higher "spousal allowance" if the income allowed is not sufficient to maintain your home or the basic necessities. Follow the same appeal procedure. If you need to appeal, contact the local Medicaid office.

What if Medicaid places a lien on my property?

A state may place a lien on your property in order to recover funds that were spent by Medicaid for your care. In fact, California recently liened 400 homes of Medicaid recipients and is continuing to lien property.

There are some strategies that may help you avoid having a lien placed on your property. Here are the details:

	IDEAS FOR REDUCING EXPOSURE OF YOUR ESTATE TO A MEDICAID LIEN
1	Ask your doctor to draft what is known as "a letter of intent". This basic document states that your doctor feels that you will be returning to the home. If it is believed that you will be returning to the home, it is one way to avoid the lien. This is a critical point in the decision of where your final days should be spent. If you come back home to die, it could possibly alleviate the home from being liened.
2	A lien on a house may be avoided if there is a spouse or child of the Medicaid recipient who is under 21 years old or disabled or blind and disabled. You may be able to prove a case that other children over age 21, brothers and sisters and parents need the home and avoid a lien.
3	By creating certain irrevocable trusts for the home, giving away the home prior to the 36 look-back rule may be a useful way to get the home out of your estate. Many elder-care experts are absolutely opposed to ever selling, gifting, or transferring the personal residence. Before making any transfer get competent, specific advice from a professional in your area. Also do not consider transferring the home within the 36 months of entering a nursing home as it could cause disqualification.
4	If a home is in fact liened, you may consider suing and seeking injunctive relief. In fact, many of the 400 liens in California were withdrawn when the current homeowners did just this. The homeowners suggested that the placement of the liens denied them due process. The district court held that the placing of the liens constituted a taking of property, requiring an opportunity for a preattachment hearing.

Some strategies for getting into the facility of your choice

Long before you apply for Medicaid you will be searching for a care facility. One of the first questions you should ask is whether the facility accepts private pay and Medicaid beneficiaries. If you enter a facility as a Medicaid patient, you will probably have to go to the facility that has the first available bed, not your first choice.

The second question to ask the nursing home is how much money you need to enter the facility as a private payer. Sometimes care facilities want to see a certain income or asset ratio or specific dollar amount. Other times, a private-pay patient will be required to pay for a certain number of months in advance. It's likely you would get into the facility of your choice as a private payer since there are more beds for the private payers. When you call a facility and ask if there is a bed available, you should not be asked whether you are a private payer or a Medicaid patient. If you think that you're being refused a bed because you're on Medicaid, contact an elder-care group in your community for help.

Don't fill out an application for a care facility haphazardly. First, you should find out the rules for admission to a particular home. Call ahead anonymously or ask an advisor to make the call to find out the admission requirements. When you fill out the application, don't offer any more information than is asked for. You may want an advisor to help you fill out the application because it will probably also be reviewed by Medicaid when you apply for Medicaid benefits in the future.

Once you're in a facility, if your money runs out, you can usually stay in the facility and transfer payment to Medicaid. Instances in which patients are transferred to other facilities because the patients are now Medicaid recipients are rare and in some instances, illegal. If a care facility says that you or a relative will be discharged, you should consider playing hardball. Tell the administrator of the hospital that you will be contacting the local Ombudsman, the Health Care Financing Administration, the local Area Agency on Aging, your attorney and the media. Ask politely for the exact time of the discharge and whether the patient will be left in the parking lot. Explain that you want to be sure you know exactly where the patient will be so that you can inform the media and your attorney.

You should understand that, as a patient, you have certain rights. To find out about these rights, ask a care facility or a long-term advocacy group, such as the Legal Counsel for the Elderly or the National Coalition for Nursing Home Reform. (Use Appendix 1 for further guidance.)

In summary, it may be a more prudent move to leave enough money liquid and assessable to get into the facility of your choice as a private payer than to wait for Medicaid.

My views of the future of our health care system

There is no question that medical benefits are being reduced, cut and in many cases, eliminated.

As I'm writing this in the spring of 1995, the newer political forces in Washington are talking about further cuts to Medicaid and also to Social Security. If these changes become the law, it's quite likely that wealthy individuals—anyone earning more than $40,000 annually—will not be entitled to Social Security. You'll pay higher Social Security and Medicare taxes, but you may only be eligible for benefits at age 70.

It's a little known fact that Social Security is actually the one entitlement program that is not a drain on the budget. The Social Security Administration keeps its funds in a separate trust account and uses its reserves to pay people their benefits. The benefits aren't included in the national budget. But you continue to read about how the "entitlement" programs" are the single leading cause of the national deficit. This is not true. Social Security should be part of this budget discussion. I'm especially worried because if Washington is trying to cut Social Security benefits—part of a solvent program—what will happen to some of the other entitlement programs that are desperately needed by the less fortunate?

There have already been so many cuts in Medicare benefits over the past few years, now Medicare is known as a "stabilization program." If you have a problem that is medically necessary, you will probably receive some type of care for a very limited amount of time. As soon as you are "stabilized," your Medicare benefit will be eliminated.

The proposed changes in the Medicaid law would also restrict benefits for necessary care as well. Although people on welfare are "rewarded" and receive more money when they have more children, Alzheimer's or stroke victims have few sources of funds. Medicaid makes it difficult to give away your money and even more difficult to shelter it. As our life expectancies increase, this problem is only going to worsen. Inevitably, all of us, including the lawmakers, are likely to procrastinate addressing this issue until it is even more of a national crisis than it is today.

I consider myself fairly conservative, but I'm very angry that you and I paid into a system and now may get nothing back. The Social Security and Medicare/Medicaid concept is good and important. The problems with the system stem from improper spending, investing and political grandstanding.

To fix the system, the lawmakers try to Band-Aid the situation, cover it up, raise taxes or penalize those who pay their taxes in order to make it work. If our elected officials did their jobs properly, I believe that every taxpayer would have some level of care and some choice in the type of care. Here are my proposals to improve the system:

1. Give individuals a choice as to how their Social Security and Medicare taxes are deducted. Let people choose to have them deducted through FICA and administered by the Social Security Administration just as it is now. Or, let people take what would be the amount of Social Security and Medicare taxes and "self-direct it" to invest on their own, following certain guidelines such as those applying to Individual Retirement Accounts. The average person would have far more money using this system. This type of system would make individuals richer and actually increase Social Security retirement income, allowing a higher allocation to Medicare and Medicaid programs to ensure every person has basic medical and long-term care benefits without having to go broke.

2. There is currently several years reserve in both the Social Security and Medicare trust funds. This amount of reserve could produce a great deal more surplus which could help other programs such as Medicaid. If the money was invested and earned an annual average return of 9 percent, the amount of money raised would fund the system for several more years.

3. Completely revamp the Medicare system from the ground up. Stiffer penalties are needed for those who defraud Medicare. Higher doctor, hospital and insurance company fees are needed. This would help raise additional money without losing millions to fraud and thus would save millions or even billions of dollars every year.

4. Institute more preventative maintenance programs. There's no reason to wait until people are ill and need serious medical attention. For example, if people received routine heart exams, many bypass surgeries would be avoided.

5. Why are we offering other countries aid when we can't even help our own citizens? We should aim to have a basic standard of living for all Americans before we provide aid to foreign countries.

6. Never take away the rights of a person as long as that person is not harming someone else. Cigarettes should not be banned. However, a sizable tobacco tax should be levied with a large portion of the tax going to the Medicare/Medicaid system. Some of the tax

should also be used for preventive educational programs that teach people the dangers of smoking. Similar programs should be used for alcohol and other potentially harmful products.

Our laws are complicated. Just as people who don't understand the tax code pay too much in taxes, those who do not understand the Social Security and Medicare system will not receive all they are entitled to. People who believe they will be taken care of in the event of a long-term illness are sadly mistaken. *Caveat emptor! Let the buyer beware.* We are the buyers. Our system does not protect us. In fact, it can harm us if we don't understand how to use it.

Some final pointers on Medicaid

While this book has provided a solid overview of the system, it's up to you to put this information to good use by planning.

Planning is so critical. You must understand what you are trying to accomplish. Medicaid requires even more careful planning because, while you accomplish one objective, you may impact another part of your financial life. Here are some additional pointers:

Gifting

One problem with a gift is the nature of a gift. By giving a gift, your heirs will have to pay a capital gains tax if there is appreciation based on the price you paid. If your beneficiaries were to receive the same asset as an inheritance, the full value "steps up" to whatever the fair market value is at the time of your death. Thus, your heirs can sell the asset at fair value at the time of your death and potentially save thousands in capital gains taxes. If for example, your home has appreciated in value by $100,000, your heirs could owe more than $30,000 in taxes.

Other tax considerations

Often, you will need to sell securities and other investments to pay for medical benefits. Sometimes, you incur capital gains when selling an investment. To balance out these gains, make sure you are absolutely maximizing all the medical deductions possible. This is one of the most overlooked deductions on tax returns.

Where to live during retirement

When you think about where you're going to live during retirement, you're probably thinking of something entirely different than what I have in mind. You probably consider factors such as weather, recreational activities, etc. I would want to know what type of state it is for Medicaid purposes.

If you move to a different state during your retirement, you should carefully consider whether you want your full-time residence in that state or not. Where you reside at the time you become ill has an impact on the benefits you'll receive.

Summary

The tangled web of changing rules and regulations of Medicaid are difficult to manage, but it's essential that you and your family deal with these issues ahead of time, before you end up in a unpleasant situation that can't be changed. The Medicaid application process can be a nightmare because of all the documentation that you will be required to provide. Then, if your application is denied, it's up to you to reapply and present your case to an appeals board. Fortunately, you can get some help from elder-care specialists. There is likely to be some Medicaid reform in the near future. Unfortunately, reform is not likely to make the process any smoother, nor will it guarantee an increase in benefits. A more drastic overhaul of the entire Medicaid system is needed for that.

Chapter 14

Power of attorney and other critical documents

Conservatorship

When creating an estate plan or elder care plan, you often plan for a death, but rarely do you plan for an incapacity. In fact, the probate courts are extremely busy, not because of transferring assets after a death, but because of conservatorship issues. It's actually quite common for assets to be frozen. If someone is not appointed in advance to administer an estate, a court will decide who will take control over the affairs of someone who can't handle them. The person with this control is a conservator. Ideally, you want to select someone to be your conservator, rather than allow the court to name someone.

Assets held as joint tenant between spouses are often needlessly frozen

You'd be surprised how easily assets can become frozen. Let's assume you own a home as joint tenant with your spouse. Your spouse is in an accident, has a stroke or is otherwise left incapacitated. It's unlikely that you'll be able to sell or refinance your house because you would only be able to provide one signature. Since the property is held in joint tenancy, both your signature and that of your spouse are needed for transactions. This rule applies to other assets held jointly such as brokerage holdings, bank accounts, etc. If you don't plan ahead, these assets will be frozen and you won't be able to do what you want with the assets. The court will decide how your assets should be disposed and you may not be happy with the court's decision. Not only will you have to get legal representation, you could miss key opportunities while your assets are frozen. You may want to sell your house but lose the prospective buyer because you can't sell it. Or, you may lose out on lower interest rates for refinancing.

Power of attorney

An excellent document to help you handle conservator problems or other loss of control issues is a power of attorney. A power of attorney lets you designate someone as your agent or attorney-in-fact to act in place of you (the principal). You can name someone power of attorney to manage specific affairs such as selling your house or general affairs, to handle a wide range of financial duties. Even more valuable is what is known as a durable power of attorney (DA). This arrangement is similar to a regular power of attorney with one exception: Most powers of attorney under common law are nullified or terminated when someone becomes incapacitated. Durable powers of attorney remain valid even when someone becomes incapacitated.

There are several ways to structure a DA arrangement. You should make an arrangement that you're comfortable with and that meets your needs. For example, a springing durable power of attorney would state that the attorney-in-fact's powers are inactive until the principal becomes incapacitated.

In addition, powers of attorney are very effective for health reasons. Few of you have what is called a durable power of attorney for health. Most states and hospitals recognize health care agents who can make medical decisions on your behalf. The agent can authorize medical treatment or without permission for a procedure. Often, if you do not have an appointed health care agent, the state will act according to law. Your wishes may not coincide with the state guidelines, so it's in your best interest to designate a health care agent.

There are some drawbacks to powers of attorney. They can become outdated and as your situation changes, the people you do business with may question the validity of the power of attorney. In some states, the document naming your agent expires after a set number of years. To avoid any disputes over your designation, you should annually resign and redate your power of attorney form. Also, immediately after you create a power of attorney, deliver it to your banks, brokerages, title companies and other firms with which you do business. Ask for a written letter that acknowledges your power of attorney and states that the firm will accept it. Just because you have a power of attorney does not mean a bank or brokerage firm will honor it. Get the acceptance in writing in advance. (See Appendix 2 for a sample of a durable power of attorney).

Who should be the agent for your durable power of attorney?

Whether you're creating a power of attorney for health or financial reasons, you should choose someone you feel is responsible and capable of making decisions for you. He or she will have a great deal of power and will control your money, investments and decisions whether you should have surgery. Use the following checklists to assist you in deciding who to name.

When you choose your health care agent, remember that certain people cannot be your agent, including your primary physician and the operator or employees of the care facility.

When you create a power of attorney for health care, you can give the agent broad or limited powers. Generally, you should give broad powers since you don't know what contingencies can arise in the future. With broad powers, the agent would be responsible for tasks including:

- The authority to accept, refuse or withdraw consent for a medical procedure.

- The right to hire and fire your medical professionals.

- The right to decide where and when to admit or withdraw you from health-care facilities.

- Access to all your medical records.

A durable power of attorney for financial affairs can be as broad or specific as needed. You might make the DA applicable to only one asset, such as your home, or you can limit the agent's power, perhaps prohibiting the sale of your home for less than a specific amount of money. When you create the document, you should draw it up carefully to make certain the agent has the powers you want him or her to have.

How long does a durable power of attorney last?

You can usually revoke a DA whenever you want as long as you are of sound mind and body. However, if you are deemed incapacitated, you may not be able to revoke the DA. Some states nullify a health care DA after five or seven years. If you do revoke a DA, you should notify all interested parties that you have changed or revoked the document.

A good strategy is to resign and reinitial your document annually and add a statement saying that your wishes are unchanged. When you resign and redate a power of attorney annually, it will be less likely that anyone will be able to question your wishes.

What if you do not want to name a power of attorney?

If there's no one you would trust to handle your financial affairs, you should consider naming the trust department of a bank or a trust company as your power of attorney. Unfortunately, this can get expensive because the trust company generally takes from 1 to 3 percent of your assets to serve as the trustee. In addition, you will be charged fees to have the trustee pay the bills, complete your tax return and manage your assets. There may also be an exit charge. In addition, when the trustee hires someone to work on your assets, such as a bookkeeper, the trustee can charge you double what the bookkeeper charges the trustee.

Still, if there's no one else to handle your affairs, you should appoint a corporate trustee. Do your research ahead of time and check all the fees before hiring a trust.

Do all financial institutions accept durable power of attorney?

Some banks or brokerages may not accept an agent's signature to handle your affairs. You should contact all the financial institutions that you deal with and ask what the procedure is for having a power of attorney handle your affairs. Meet with the manager of your bank, brokerage and other companies and get written acceptance letters.

The proper way to designate a durable power of attorney

1. When you create a durable power of attorney, make sure you sign it, date it and have the required number of eligible witnesses also sign it. If a notary is required, make certain he or she signs the document and records the notarization in his or her record log.

2. Find out how and when you must record the document in court.

3. Check that the document has provisions for the durable power of attorney to continue if you become incapacitated.

4. Choose a competent and trustworthy attorney-in-fact. You should appoint a contingency attorney-in-fact if your first choice is unable to represent you.

MAXIMUM FAMILY BENEFITS FOR 1995

MONTHLY MAXIMUM	INDIVIDUAL	COUPLE
Basic Federal Payment:	$458	$687
Income Limits: With Earned Income: With Unearned Income:	$1,001 478	$1,459 707
Asset Limits (Annual):	$2,000	$3,000

MAIN REQUIREMENTS FOR SSI ELIGIBILITY

1	AGE	You must be (A) 65 years of age or older, or (B) blind, or (C) disabled. The definition of an adult who is disabled is very similar to Disability Definition for Social Security Disability Insurance benefits (see explanation). To determine if a child (under age 18) is eligible is defined as, "any medically determinable physical or mental impairment of comparable severity (to that of an adult)". Basically, they are looking to see if you can function independently, appropriately, and effectively in an age-appropriate manner.
2	MEDICAL CONDITION	You may qualify if you are blind (defined the same for SS Disability Insurance).
3	CITIZENSHIP AND RESIDENCY REQUIREMENTS	You must be living in the United States (including Washington D.C., Northern Mariana Islands, but not Puerto Rico). You must also be a citizen of the United States, or an alien lawfully admitted for permanent residence or permanently residing in the United States (under that legal definition).
4	INCOME AND ASSET TEST	This is a discussion in and of itself. Basically, you have countable income (and income not counted), as well as countable assets. In 1994, singles are allowed countable earned income up to $977, or $466 of unearned income, per month. A couple living alone, in a private household is allowed to earn (of earned income) $1,423, or $689 of unearned income. In terms of assets (or they like to use the word "resources") you are allowed for individuals, $2,000 or less; for married, $3,000 or less.

Advanced directives and living wills

The advances of medical science have brought to the forefront the issue of an individual's right to decide whether to have life support or other extra-ordinary means to prolong life.

This issue is a sensitive one. Prolonging one's life can be a financial drain on the family, as well as a severe emotional strain. To address some of these concerns, you can write an advanced directive. This written document states the type of medical procedures you want used or not used to keep yourself alive. The document spells out what measures you wish to be taken.

The Patient Self Determination Act (PSDA) is effective for services provided on or after December 1, 1991. This Act amends certain Medicare and Medicaid provisions in the Social Security Act to encourage use of advance directives. A person can control his or her health-care decisions after becoming incapacitated. Medicare and Medicaid providers are required to give all patients written information on state laws regarding advanced directives at the time of admission to an institution.

The type or extent of advanced directives is primarily governed by state law.

Living will

With regard to advanced directives, living wills are essential documents. Living wills allow you to specify wishes in advance about measures you want taken. Most state that if you become terminally ill, you don't want any heroic measures taken or any life-support systems used to prolong your death.

The sample living will on page 143 is not meant to be a legal document. All states have different requirements on the validity of a living will. Consult your advisers for a living will that is valid where you live.

When creating an advanced directive, be it a DPA or living will, follow these steps:

1. **Follow state law.** Roughly 47 states recognize living wills, and 48 states recognize DPA for health care. Rules and requirements vary by state; some states want two nonfamily witnesses while other states prefer a notary as a witness.

2. **Make copies of your advanced directives.** Give a copy to your primary care physician for your central medical file. Put a copy with your safe papers, preferably in a safe-deposit box and leave a copy in your home. You may even want to carry a mini-copy with you in case of an emergency.

3. Update regularly. Some states have a time limit on the validity of advanced directives. You should regularly review them and make any necessary changes. Even if you don't make changes, consider resigning and redating the document to keep the directives fresh.

A living will (directive to physicians)

If I should have an incurable and irreversible condition that has been diagnosed by two physicians and that will result in my death within a relatively short period of time without the administration of life-sustaining treatment or has produced an irreversible coma or persistent vegetative state, and I am no longer able to make decisions regarding my medical treatment, I direct my attending physician, pursuant to the Natural Death Act of California, to withhold or withdraw treatment, including artificially administered nutrition and hydration that only prolongs the process of dying or the irreversible coma or persistent vegetative state and is not necessary for my comfort or to alleviate pain.

Dated: _____

Name: _____

Signature: _____

The declarant voluntarily signed this writing in my presence. I am not a health care provider, an employee of a health care provider, the operator of a community care facility, an employee of an operator of a community care facility, the operator of a residential care facility for the elderly or an employee of an operator of a residential care facility for the elderly.

Signature: _____

Address: _____

_____

Witness 1: _____

Date: _____

Signature: _____

Address: _____

_____

Witness 2: _____

Date: _____

There is no doubt that advanced directives make tremendous sense. Don't be intimidated by medical professionals who may not know the rules on these directives. Although Medicare and Medicaid standards require personnel to give you information about advanced directives, often they don't. It's crucial that you get professional help preparing the documents ahead of time. Once life support and similar measures are taken, it is very difficult to undue these measures.

Summary

You have the power to protect your assets if you should become disabled or otherwise incapacitated. You have to use this power, however, before you are disabled. To make certain that sound decisions are made on your behalf, you should use a power of attorney that allows the person of your choice to make financial and legal decisions. The person can have a limited power of attorney or a more extensive one, granting him or her decision-making power in all aspects of your life. In addition to a power of attorney, you should have a living will to specify what medical treatments you want used if you become terminally ill. Seek counsel if you have questions about your care or your financial matters.

Chapter 15

Nursing home advocacy and patients' rights

The Older Americans Act

In 1973 and again in 1978, laws were passed that established and commissioned the Area Agency on Aging. This agency is the authorized advocate for the elderly. Through this agency, you can find services such as Legal Assistance, the Ombudsman program to survey nursing homes, job training programs, transportation services and nutrition programs.

Federal Nursing Home Reform Act (NHRA)

This legislation became effective as part of the Omnibus Reconciliation Act of 1987, but many of the amendments and provisions became effective as of October 1990. This legislation has been instrumental in improving the standard of care and quality of life for nursing home residents.

The goal of the NHRA is to insure that residents have the right and the knowledge that they are entitled to the highest possible physical, mental and psychosocial well-being. The NHRA places more stringent requirements on nursing homes, requiring further training and certification of nurses and aides.

It is this Act that makes discrimination against Medicaid recipients illegal. The act says that Medicaid recipients should enjoy the same quality care as non-Medicaid recipients. The law states that when a client applies to a nursing home, the care facility should not ask if the recipient is a private payer or on Medicaid.

Hill-Burton Act

This Act provided Federal construction loans and other assistance programs to build homes. The nursing homes that have received this Federal aid may be required to make certain services available to those who would otherwise be unable to pay for them. If one of these facilities doesn't admit a Medicare or Medicaid recipient, the patient should file a complaint or lawsuit.

Handling nursing home complaints

Every nursing home is required to post a written list of the patient's rights. If you have a grievance with a nursing home, talk to the nursing home administrator. The administrator is required to take prompt steps to resolve the grievance. Don't be intimidated by the nursing home staff. Say that you will write to the local Area Agency on Aging, local Ombudsman office, Health Care Financing Administration, the state bar, the media and other advocacy groups in order to resolve your grievance.

It is the job of the local Ombudsman to investigate and resolve complaints. The Ombudsman will review how a nursing facility has corrected the problem and whether the resolution adheres to the local, state and Federal laws.

Getting expert help

Help is available for whatever problem you face, so you shouldn't have to take on the battle alone. There are free legal services, as well as toll-free hotlines. Here are some suggestions:

1. Spend a day contacting all the help agencies from the elder-care hotline to the Area Agency on Aging, local senior centers and any other agencies that may be able to help you.

2. Contact trusted friends and advisers, including accountants, financial planners and attorneys.

3. Remember that senior citizens are entitled to some free legal help. Contact your local Bar Association or Area Agency on Aging for help.

4. If you decide to use an attorney, interview at least three lawyers. Ask them for references. When you contact the references, ask whether the attorneys successfully handled the problems and whether the client was satisfied with the level of service. Always find out the fees before hiring an attorney. If you need help finding an elder-care attorney, you can contact the National Academy of Elder-Care Attorneys at 602-881-4005.

Appendix 1

Important resources and help agencies

Medicare Hotline

Special numbers are available to answer Medicare questions. The numbers: 1-800-234-5772 and 1-800-638-6833. All Medicare questions about insurance, supplements, co-payments, to how to sign up for the Medicare Qualified Beneficiary Program will be answered. Operators will also tell you who your local insurance carrier is.

Peer Review Organization

These groups are responsible for monitoring medical payments, watching doctors to insure they perform in an ethical fashion and review the quality of care given to Medicare recipients. This group has the right to deny claims by individuals, etc. (See Appendix 3 for a complete list of PROs by state).

Health Care Financing Administration

This agency is a good source of information on Medicare, Medicaid, supplements and related subjects.

200 Independence Ave. SW
Washington, DC 20201
1-800-638-6833, 202-690-6726

Health Insurance Association of America

This industry association can provide information and free brochures on health insurance. You can call the toll-free number: 1-800-942-4242.

Eldercare Locator

This new service is run in part by the National Association for Area Agencies on Aging. It is designed to find specific local agencies and organizations that can provide you assistance or specific programs in your community such as Meals on Wheels, free insurance counseling, legal services, etc. The number to call is 1-800-677-1116.

Consumer Information Center

Part of the General Services Administration, this center publishes a wide range of publications on Social Security and other Federal programs.

P.O. Box 100
Pueblo, CO 81002
719-948-3334

Social Security and Medicare Legal Counsel

Center for Law and Social Policy

This agency is a nonprofit public interest law firm which represents minorities, the poor and the disabled. Assistance is given for child support matters, job retraining, family law, health care and other issues.

1616 P Street NW, Suite 450
Washington, DC 20036
202-328-5140
Fax: 202-328-5195

Center On Social Welfare Policy and Law

This is a national support center dealing with issues involving public assistance programs such as Aid to Families with Dependent Children and Supplemental Security Income. The center will provide referrals to local legal groups and provide help for people seeking public assistance.

275 Seventh Ave., 6th Fl.
New York, NY 10001
212-633-6967
Fax: 212-633-6371

1029 Vermont Ave. NW, Suite 850
Washington, DC 20005
202-347-5615
Fax: 202-347-5462

Mental Health Law Project

This project works primarily with the rights of the developmentally and mentally disabled by assisting in legal matters, counseling and training.

1101 15th St. NW, Suite 1212
Washington, DC 20005
202-467-5730
Fax: 202-223-0409

National Consumer Law Center

This Law Center works as a support center for consumer and energy related issues for people with low incomes. It provides referrals to attorneys and provides newsletters and publications on consumer and energy law.

11 Beacon St., Suite 821
Boston, MA 02108
617-523-8010

1875 Connecticut Ave. NW
Washington, DC 20009
202-986-6060
Fax: 202-986-6648

National Health Law Program

This program provides low income clients better access to quality health care. Help includes litigation assistance, technical advice and training. A quarterly newsletter is published.

2639 S. La Cienega Blvd.
Los Angeles, CA 90034
310-204-6010
Fax: 310-204-0891

1815 H St. NW
Suite 700
Washington, DC 20006
202-785-6792

National Organization of Social Security Claimants' Representatives

This a membership organization working on behalf of Social Security claimants and beneficiaries. It sponsors an annual conference.

6 Prospect St.
Midland Park, NJ 07432
201-444-1415
Fax: 201-444-1823

National Senior Citizens Law Center

This is a support center providing assistance and information to advocates on legal problems for the aged. It monitors administrative and legislative proposals and keep attorneys informed of new developments in issues such as age discrimination, government benefits, private pensions, nursing homes and private pensions.

1815 H St. NW, Suite 700	1052 West Sixth St., 7th Fl.
Washington, DC 20006	Los Angeles, CA 90017
202-887-5280	213-482-3550
Fax: 202-785-6972	Fax: 213-482-8009

Area agencies on aging

Administered by the Administration on Aging and headed by the Assistant Secretary for Aging in the Department of Health and Human Services, these organizations are an excellent resource to help you find local senior centers, hospice care providers, legal help, etc. The job training program is especially helpful. Look in your phone book for your local Area Agency on Aging. (See Appendix 3 for the main location in your state.)

State insurance commissioner

Many states have special programs for seniors including partnerships for long-term care designed to help you protect your money from a long-term care spend-down. Many states have senior divisions for help, fraud prevention, etc. Contact your local insurance commissioner.

Local senior centers

Usually listed at the beginning of phone books, local senior centers can be invaluable tools. Many offer workshops, social programs and support groups. Through these meetings, you're likely to meet people who have faced the problems you're having.

Veterans Administration

Call 1-800-827-1000 for information on veterans benefits and survivor benefits.

National Committee to Preserve Social Security and Medicare

Although you may not agree with this group's position, this is a much needed watchdog organization. The group offers information and lets you express your opinion of Social Security.

2000 K St. NW, Suite 800
Washington, DC 20006
202-822-9459

Additional resources

American Association of Homes
for the Aging (AAHA)
1050 17th St.
Washington, DC 20036

Nat'l Association for Home Care
519 C St. NE
Washington, DC 20002
202-547-7424

Help for hearing disabilities

National Captioning Institute
5203 Leesburg Pike
Falls Church, VA 22041

The Lions Club International
300 22nd St.
Oak Brook, IL 60570

Alexander Graham Bell Association for
the Deaf
3417 Volta Place NW
Washington, DC 20007

American Foundation for the Blind
15 W. 16th St.
New York, NY 10011

Legal assistance

American Bar Association Commission On
Legal Problems for the Elderly
1800 M St. NW, Suite 200
Washington, DC 20036

National Academy of Elder Law
Attorneys, Inc.
655 N. Alvernon, Suite 108
Tucson, AZ 85711

National Citizens Coalition for
Nursing Home Reform
(NCCNHR)
1224 M St. NW, #301
Washington, DC 20005-5183
202-393-2018

Medicare carriers by state

The 800 numbers can be used only in the states or service areas listed.

Alabama

Medicare/Blue Cross-Blue Shield of
 Alabama
450 Riverchase Pkwy.
Birmingham, AL 35298
800-292-88555, 205-988-2244

Alaska

Medicare/Aetna Life & Casualty
200 SW Market St., P.O. Box 1998
Portland, OR 97207-1998
800-452-0125, 503-222-6831

Arizona

Medicare/Aetna Life & Casualty
P.O. Box 37200
Phoenix, AZ 85069
800-772-1213, 602-861-1968

Arkansas

Medicare/Arkansas Blue Cross and
 Blue Shield—A Mutual Ins. Co.
P.O. Box 1418
Little Rock, AR 72203
800-482-5525, 501-378-2320

California

*Counties of Los Angeles, Orange, San
Diego, Ventura, Imperial, San Luis
Obispo, Santa Barbara*
Medicare/Transamerica Occidental
 Life Insurance Co.
Box 50061
Upland, CA 91785-0061
800-252-9020, 213-748-2311

Rest of state
Medicare Claims Department
Blue Shield of California
Chico, CA 95976
Northern California, 800-952-8627
816-743-1583
Riverside, San Bernardino, 800-848-7713
909-796-9393

Colorado

Medicare
P.O. Box 173500
Denver, CO 80217
800-332-6681, 303-831-2661

Connecticut

Medicare/The Travelers Insurance Co.
538 Preston Ave
P.O. Box 9000
Meriden, CT 06454-9000
800-982-6819, 203-237-8592

Delaware

Medicare/Pennsylvania Blue Shield
P.O. Box 890204
Camp Hill, PA 17089-0204
800-851-3535

District of Columbia

Medicare/Pennsylvania Blue Shield
P.O. Box 890109
Camp Hill, PA 17089-0109

Florida

Medicare Pt. B/Blue Shield of Florida
P.O. Box 2360
Jacksonville, FL 32231
800-333-7586, 904-355-3680
Short order service 800-666-7586

Georgia

Medicare Pt. B/Aetna Life & Casualty
12052 Middleground Rd., Box 3018
Savannah, GA 31402-3018
800-727-0827, 912-927-0934

Hawaii

Medicare/Aetna Life & Casualty
P.O. Box 3947
Honolulu, HI 96812
800-272-5242, 808-524-1240

Idaho

CIGNA
3150 N. Lake Harbor Lane, Suite 254
P.O. Box 8048
Boise, ID 83707
800-627-2782, 208-342-7763

Illinois

Medicare Claims
Blue Cross & Blue Shield of Illinois
P.O. Box 4422
Marion, IL 62959
800-642-6930, 312-938-8000

Indiana

Medicare AdminaStar Federal
8115 Knue Road
Indianapolis, IN 46250
800-622-4792, 317-842-4151

Iowa

Medicare/Blue Cross & Blue Shield
   of Iowa
636 Grand Ave
Des Moines, IA 50309
800-532-1285, 515-245-4785

Kansas

Counties of Johnson, Wyandotte
Medicare/Blue Cross & Blue Shield
   of Kansas
P.O. Box 239
Topeka, KS 66601
800-432-3531, 816-561-0900

Rest of state
Medicare/Blue Cross & Blue Shield
   of Kansas
1133 SW Topeka Blvd.
Topeka, KS 66629
800-432-3531, 913-232-3773

Kentucky

Medicare Part B
Blue Cross & Blue Shield of Kentucky
100 E. Vine St.
Lexington, KY 40507
800-999-7608, 606-233-1441

Louisiana

Medicare Services/Arkansas Blue
   Cross & Blue Shield
P.O. Box 83810
Baton Rouge, LA 70884-3810
800-462-9666
New Orleans, 504-529-1494
Baton Rouge, 504-927-3490

Maine

C&S Admin. Services Medicare
P.O. Box 100
Hingham, MA 02044-9191
800-492-0919, 207-828-4300

Maryland

Montgomery, Prince George's counties
Medicare Pt. B/Pennsylvania Blue Shield
1800 Center St., P.O. Box 890108
Camp Hill, PA 17089-1124
All states, 800-233-1124

Rest of state
Medicare/Maryland Blue Shield Inc.
1946 Greenspring Dr.
Timonium, MD 21093
800-492-4795, 410-561-4160

Massachusetts

Medicare/Blue Shield of Massachusetts
P.O. Box 100
Hingham, MA 02044
800-882-1228, 617-741-3300

Michigan

Medicare Part B
Blue Cross & Blue Shield of Michigan
P.O. Box 2201 Dept. 0417
Detroit, MI 48231-2201
Area codes 313, 517, 616:
800-482-4045
Area code 906: 800-562-7884
In Detroit, 313-225-8200

Minnesota

Counties of Anoka, Dakota, Filmore,
Goodhue, Hennepin, Houston, Olmstead,
Ramsey, Wabasha, Washington, Winona
Medicare/The Travelers Ins. Co.
8120 Penn Ave. S.
Bloomington, MN 55431
800-352-2762, 612-884-7171

Rest of state
Medicare Pt. B/Blue Cross & Blue
   Shield of Minnesota
3525 Blue Cross Road.
P.O. Box 64357
St. Paul MN 55164
All states, 800-382-2000, 612-456-5070

Mississippi

Medicare/The Travelers Ins Co.
705 Woodlands Pkwy., P.O. Box 22545
Jackson, MS 39225-2545
800-682-5417
Outside state, 800-227-2349
601-956-0372

Missouri

Counties of Andrew, Atchison, Bates,
Benton, Buchanan, Caldwell, Carroll,
Cass, Clay, Clinton, Daviess, DeKalb,
Gentry, Grundy, Harison, Henry, Holt,
Jackson, Johnson, Lafayette, Livingston,
Mercer, Nodaway, Pettis, Platte, Ray, St.
Clair, Saline, Vernon, Worth
Medicare/Blue Cross & Blue Shield
   of Kansas
P.O. Box 419840
Kansas City, MO 64108-6840
800-892-5900, 816-561-0900

Rest of state

Medicare/General American Life Ins. Co.
13045 Pesson Ferry Road, Box 505
St. Louis, MO 63128
800-392-3070, 314-843-8880

Montana

Medicare/Blue Cross & Blue Shield
of Montana
2501 Beltview Dr., P.O. Box 4310
Helena, MT 59604
800-332-6146, 406-444-8350

Nebraska

Medicare Part B
Blue Cross & Blue Shield of Nebraska
7261 Mercy Road
Omaha, NE 68180-0001
800-633-1113, 402-390-1800

Nevada

Medicare/Aetna Life & Casualty
P.O. Box 37230
Phoenix, AZ 85069
800-528-0311, 602-861-1968

New Hampshire

Medicare Pt B/Blue Shield of
Massachusetts/Tri-State
2 1/2 Beacon St.
Concord, NH 03301
800-447-1141, 207-828-4300

New Jersey

Medicare/Pennsylvania Blue Shield
P.O. Box 400050
Harrisburg, PA 17140-0050
800-462-9306, 717-975-7333

New Mexico

Medicare/Aetna Life Insurance Co.
P.O. Box 25500
Oklahoma City, OK 73125-0500
800-423-2925, 505-821-3350

New York

*Counties of Bronx, Columbia, Dela-
ware, Duchess, Greene, Kings, Nassau,
New York, Orange, Putnam, Richmond, Rockland, Suffolk, Sullivan,
Ulster, Westchester*

Medicare B/Empire Blue Cross & Blue
Shield
P.O. Box 2280
Peekskill, NY 10566
800-442-8430, 516-244-5100

Queens County

Medicare/Group Health Inc.
P.O. Box 1608 Ansonia Station
New York, NY 10023
212-721-1770

Rest of state

Upstate Medicare Division—Pt. B
Blue Shield of Western New York
7-9 Court St.
Binghamton, NY 13901-3197
800-252-6550, 607-772-6906

North Carolina

Connecticut General Life Insurance
Company
P.O. Box 671
Nashville, TN 37202
800-672-3071, 910-665-0348

North Dakota

Medicare/Blue Shield of North Dakota
4510 13th Ave. SW
Fargo, ND 58121-0001
800-247-2267, 701-282-0691

Ohio

Medicare/Nationwide Mutual Ins. Co.
P.O. Box 57
Columbus, OH 43216
800-282-0530, 614-249-7157

Oklahoma

Medicare/Aetna Life Insurance Co.
701 NW 63rd St.
Oklahoma City, OK 73116-7693
800-522-9079, 405-848-7711

Oregon

Medicare/Aetna Life Insurance Co.
200 SW Market St., P.O. Box 1997
Portland, OR 97207-1997
800-452-0125, 503-222-6831

Pennsylvania

Medicare/Pennsylvania Blue Shield
1800 Center St.
Camp Hill, PA 17089-0065
800-382-1274, 717-763-3601

Rhode Island

Medicare/Blue Cross & Blue Shield
    of Rhode Island
Inquiry Dept.
444 Westminster St.
Providence, RI 02903-3279
800-662-5170, 401-861-2273

South Carolina

Medicare Part B/Blue Cross & Blue
    Shield of South Carolina
P.O. Box 100190
Columbia, SC 29202
All states, 800-868-2522, 803-788-3882

South Dakota

Medicare/Blue Shield of North Dakota
4510 13th Ave. SW
Fargo, ND 58121-0001
800-437-4762, 701-282-0691

Tennessee

Medicare Part B/CIGNA
P.O. Box 1465
Nashville, TN 37202
800-342-8900, 615-244-5650

Texas

Medicare/Blue Cross & Blue Shield
    of Texas, Inc.
P.O. Box 660031
Dallas, TX 75266-0031
800-442-2620, 214-235-3433

Utah

Medicare/Blue Shield of Utah
P.O. Box 30269
Salt Lake City, UT 84120-0269
800-426-3477, 801-481-6196

Vermont

Medicare/C&S Administrative Services
P.O. Box 100
Hingham, MA 02044-9191
800-447-1142, 207-828-4300

Virginia

Counties of Arlington, Fairfax
Medicare/Pennsylvania Blue Shield
P.O. Box 890100
Camp Hill, PA 17089-0100
800-233-1124, 717-763-3601

Rest of state
Medicare/The Travelers Insurance
  Company
P.O. Box 26463
Richmond, VA 23261
800-552-3423, 804-330-4786

Washington

Medicare
King County Medical Blue Shield
P.O. Box 91070
Seattle, WA 98111-3248
800-422-4087
Seattle, 206-464-3711
Tacoma, 206-597-6530

West Virginia

Medicare/Nationwide Mutual Insurance
P.O. Box 57
Columbus, OH 43216
800-848-0106, 614-249-7157

Wisconsin

Medicare/WPS
P.O. Box 1787
Madison, WI 53701
800-944-0051
In Madison, 608-221-3330

Wyoming

Blue Cross & Blue Shield of North
  Dakota
P.O. Box 628
Cheyenne, WY 82003
800-442-2371, 307-632-9381

American Samoa

Medicare/Aetna Life Insurance Co.
P.O. Box 3947
Honolulu, HI 96812
808-524-1240

Guam

Medicare/Aetna Life Insurance Co.
P.O. Box 3947
Honolulu, HI 96812
808-524-1240

Northern Mariana Islands

Medicare/Aetna Life Insurance Co.
P.O. Box 3947
Honolulu, HI 96812
808-524-1240

Puerto Rico

Medicare/Seguros de Sevicio de
  Salud de Puerto Rico
Call Box 71391
San Juan, PR 00936
Puerto Rico, 800-462-7015
Puerto Rico metro area, 809-749-4900

Virgin Islands

Medicare/Seguros de Servicio de
  Salud de Puerto Rico
Call Box 71391
San Juan, PR 00936
800-474-7448

Summary

You've worked hard to help your family and now you hope to enjoy your retirement. To lose your resources in a degrading manner because of serious illness is simply ludicrous. Part of the problem is our system, but you and I are also at fault for believing that society will take care of us. Still, you should make the most of the benefits now available to you. Don't be intimidated by the complexity of the system. Utilize the government hotline numbers as well as the many other elder-care and legal resources available. You have to plan ahead and learn how to utilize government and private programs to their full advantage.

Appendix 2

Sample general durable power of attorney

The following are sample Durable Power of Attorney and Durable Power of Attorney for Healthcare forms. These forms are used in California; you should check with a lawyer in your state to make sure there are no other legal requirements where you live.

Sample general durable power of attorney

I, _____ principal (the "principal"), have
this day appointed _____ to serve as my
Agent ("Agent") and to exercise the powers set forth below.

If _____ shall be unable or unwilling to serve
or to continue to serve, then I appoint _____
as substitute or successor agent to serve with the same powers.

Article I

My Agent is authorized in my Agent's sole and absolute discretion
from time to time and at any time, with respect to any and all of
my property and interests in property, real, personal, intangible
and mixed, as follows:

1. With respect to real property: to sell, buy, lease, sublease,
   release; to eject, remove, and relieve tenants or other
   persons from, and recover possession of by all lawful means;
   to collect, sue for, receive and receipt for rents and profits
   and to conserve, invest, or utilize any and all of such rents,
   profits, and receipts for the purposes described in this
   paragraph; to maintain, protect, repair, preserve, insure,
   build upon, demolish, alter, or improve all or any part
   thereof;

2. With respect to personal property: to sell, buy lease,
   sublease, and release; to recover possession of by all lawful
   means; to collect, sue for, receive, and receipt for rents and
   profits therefrom; to maintain, protect, repair, preserve,
   insure, alter, or improve all or any part thereof;

3. To establish accounts of all kinds, including checking and
   savings, for me with financial institutions of any kind; to
   modify, terminate, make deposits to, and write checks on or
   make withdrawals from and grant security interests in all
   accounts in my name or with respect to which I am an
   authorized signatory whether or not any such account was
   established by me or for me by my Agent, to negotiate,
   endorse, or transfer any checks or other instruments with
   respect to any such accounts; to contract for any services
   rendered by any bank or financial institution;

4. To institute, supervise, prosecute, defend, intervene in,
   abandon, compromise, arbitrate, settle, dismiss, and appeal
   from any and all legal, equitable, judicial, or administrative

hearings, actions, suits, proceedings, attachments, arrests, or distresses, involving me in any way;

5. To represent me in all tax matters;

6. To transfer from time to time and at any time to the trustee or trustees of any revocable trust agreement created by me before or after the execution of this instrument, as to which trust I am, during my lifetime, a primary income and principal beneficiary, any and all of my cash, property, or interests in property, including any rights to receive income from any source; and for this purpose to enter and remove from any safe deposit box of mine (whether the box is registered in my name alone or jointly with one or more other persons) any of my cash or property and to execute such instruments, documents, and papers to effect the transfers described herein as may be necessary, appropriate, incidental, or convenient; to make such transfers absolutely in fee simple or for my lifetime only with the remainder of reversion (of the property so transferred) remaining in me so that such property will be disposed of at my death by my will or by the intestacy laws for the state in which I shall die a resident;

7. To support and/or continue to support any person whom I have undertaken to support or to whom I may owe an obligation of support, in the same manner and in accordance with the same standard of living as I have provided in the past, (adjusted if necessary by circumstances and inflation).

Article II

My Agent is authorized in my Agent's sole and absolute discretion from time to time and at any time, with respect to the control and management of my person, as follows:

1. To do all acts necessary for maintaining my customary standard of living; to provide living quarters by purchase, lease, or other arrangement, or by payment of the operating costs of my existing living quarters, including interest, amortization payments, repairs, and taxes; to provide normal domestic help for the operation of my household; to provide clothing, transportation, medicine, food, and incidentals; and if necessary, to make all necessary arrangements, contractual or otherwise, for me at any hospital, hospice, nursing home, convalescent home, or similar establishment;

2. To make advance arrangements for my funeral and burial.

Article III

For the purpose of inducing all persons, organizations, corporations, and entities including but not limited to any physician, hospital, bank, broker, custodian, insurer, lender, transfer agent, taxing authority, governmental agency, or party to act in accordance with the instructions of my Agent given in this instrument, I hereby represent, warrant, and agree that:

1. If this instrument is revoked or amended for any reason I, my estate, my heirs, successors, and assigns will hold any person, organization, corporation, or entity (hereinafter referred to in the aggregate as "Person") harmless from any loss suffered, or liability incurred by such Person in acting in accordance with the instructions of my Agent acting under this instrument prior to the receipt by such Person of actual notice of any such revocation or amendment.

2. The powers conferred on my Agent by this instrument may be exercised by my Agent alone and my Agent's signature or act under the authority granted in this instrument may be accepted by Persons as fully authorized by me and with the same force and effect as if I were personally present, competent, and acted on my own behalf. Consequently, all acts lawfully done by my Agent hereunder are done with my consent and shall have the same validity and effect as if I were personally present and personally exercised the powers myself, and shall inure to the benefit of and bind me and my heirs, assigns, and personal representatives.

3. No person who acts in reliance upon any representations my Agent may make as to (a) the fact that my Agent's powers are then in effect, (b) the scope of my Agent's authority granted under this instrument, (c) my competency at the time this instrument is executed, (d) the fact that his instrument has not been revoked, or (e) the fact that my Agent continues to serve as my Agent shall incur any liability to me, my estate, my heirs or assigns for permitting my Agent to exercise any such authority, nor shall any Person who deals with my Agent be responsible to determine or insure the proper application of funds or property.

Article IV

This power of attorney shall not be affected by subsequent disability or incapacity of the principal.

Article V

To the extent that I am permitted by law to do so, I herewith nominate, constitute, and appoint my Agent to serve as my guardian, conservator, and/or in any similar representative capacity, and if I am not permitted by law to so nominate, constitute, and appoint, then I request in the strongest possible terms that any court of competent jurisdiction which may receive and be asked to act upon a petition by any person to appoint a guardian, conservator, or similar representative for me the greatest possible weight to this request.

In witness whereof, I have executed this Power of Attorney this day of _____, 19_____.

_____
(Signature of Principal)

_____
Name of Principal

State of California
County of San Diego

On _____ before me, _____
        DATE   NAME, TITLE OF OFFICER

personally appeared _____

proved to me on the basis of satisfactory evidence to be the person whose name is subscribed to the within instrument and acknowledged to me that she executed the same in her authorized capacity, and that by her signature on the instrument the person, or the entity upon behalf of which the person acted, executed the instrument.

WITNESS my hand and Official Seal.

_____
NOTARY PUBLIC

The undersigned acknowledge(s) and accept(s) appointment as Agent under this instrument.

Witnesses:

_____   _____
                                (Signature of Agent)

_____   _____
                                Name of Agent

Statutory Form Durable Power of Attorney for Health Care
(California Civil Code Section 2500)

Warning to person executing this document:

This is an important legal document which is authorized by the Keene Health Care Agent Act. Before executing this document, you should know these important facts:

This document gives the person you designate as your agent (the Attorney In Fact) the power to make health care decisions for you. Your agent must act consistently with your desires as stated in this document or otherwise made known.

Except as you otherwise specify in this document, this document gives your agent the power to consent to your doctor not giving treatment or stopping treatment necessary to keep you alive.

Notwithstanding this document, you have the right to make medical and other health care decisions for yourself so long as you can give informed consent with respect to the particular decision. In addition, no treatment may be given to you over your objection at the time, and health care necessary to keep you alive may not be stopped or withheld if you object at the time.

This document gives your agent authority to consent, to refuse to consent, or to withdraw consent to any care, treatment, service, or procedure to maintain, diagnose, or treat a physical or mental condition. This power is subject to any statement of your desires and any limitations that you include in this document. You may state in this document any types of treatment that you do not desire. In addition, a court can take away the power of your agent to make health decisions for you if your agent (1) authorizes anything that is illegal, (2) acts contrary to your known desires, (3) when your desires are not known, does anything that is clearly contrary to your best interests.

The powers given by this document will exist for an indefinite period of time unless you limit their duration in this document.

You have the right to revoke the authority of your agent by notifying your agent or your treating doctor, hospital, or other health care provider orally or in writing of the revocation.

Your agent has the right to examine your medical records and to consent to their disclosure unless you limit this right in this document.

Unless you otherwise specify in this document, this document gives your agent the power after you die to (1) authorize an autopsy, (2) donate your body or parts thereof for transplant or therapeutic or educational or scientific purposes, and (3) direct the disposition of your remains.

This document revokes any prior durable power of attorney for health care.

You should carefully read and follow the witnessing procedure described at the end of this form. This document will not be valid unless you comply with the witnessing procedure.

If there is anything in this document that you do not understand, you should ask a lawyer to explain it to you.

Your agent may need this document immediately in case of an emergency that requires a decision concerning your health care. Either keep this document where it is immediately available to your agent and alternate agents or give each of them an unexecuted copy of this document. You may also want to give your doctor an executed copy of this document.

Do not use this form if you are a conservatee under the Lanterman-Petris-Short Act and you want to appoint your conservator as your agent. You can do that only if the appointment document includes a certificate of your attorney.

1. **DESIGNATION OF HEALTH CARE AGENT.** I, _____
_____, do hereby designate and appoint _____
_____, as my attorney in fact (agent) to make health care decisions for me as authorized in this document. For the purposes of this document, "health care decision" means consent, refusal of consent, or withdrawal of consent to any care, treatment, service, or procedure to maintain, diagnose, or treat an individual's physical or mental condition.

2. **CREATION OF DURABLE POWER OF ATTORNEY FOR HEALTH CARE.** By this document I intend to create a durable power of attorney for health care under Sections 2430 to 2443, inclusive, of the California Civil Code. This power of attorney shall not be affected by my subsequent incapacity.

3. **GENERAL STATEMENT OF AUTHORITY GRANTED.** Subject to any limitations in this document, I hereby grant to my agent full power and authority to make health care decisions for me to the same extent that I could make such decisions for myself if I had the capacity to do so. In exercising this authority, my agent shall make health care decisions that are consistent with my desires as stated in this document or otherwise made known to my agent, including, but not limited to, my desires concerning obtaining or

refusing or withdrawing life-prolonging care, treatment, service and procedures.

(If you want to limit the authority of your agent to make health care decisions for you, you can state the limitations in paragraph 4 ("Statement of Desires, Special Provisions, and Limitations") below. You can indicate your desires by including a statement of your desires in the same paragraph.)

4.   STATEMENT OF DESIRES, SPECIAL PROVISIONS, AND LIMITATIONS. (Your agent must make health care decisions that are consistent with your known desires. You can, but are not required to, state your desires in the space provided below. You should consider whether you want to include a statement of your desires concerning life-prolonging care, treatment, services, and procedures. You can also include a statement of your desires concerning other matters relating to your health care. You can also make your desires known to your agent by discussing your desires with your agent or by some other means. If there are any types of treatment that you do not want to be used, you should state them in the space below. If you want to limit in any other way the authority given your agent by this document, you should state the limits in the space below. If you do not state any limits, your agent will have broad powers to make health care decisions for you, except to the extent that there are limits provided by law.)

In exercising the authority under this durable power of attorney for health care, my agent shall act consistently with my desires as stated below and is subject to the special provisions and limitations stated below:

(a) Statement of desires concerning life-prolonging care, treatment, services, and procedures:

I do not want my life to be prolonged and I do not want life-sustaining treatment to be provided or continued if the burdens of the treatment outweigh the expected benefits. I want my agent to consider the relief of suffering and the quality as well as the extent of the possible extension of my life in making decisions concerning life-sustaining treatment.

(b) Additional statement of desires, special provisions, and limitations: NONE

5.   INSPECTION AND DISCLOSURE OF INFORMATION RELATING TO MY PHYSICAL OR MENTAL HEALTH. Subject to any limitations in this document, my agent has the power and authority to do all of the following:

(a) Request, review, and receive any information, verbal or written, regarding my physical or mental health, including, but not limited to, medical and hospital records.

(b) Execute on my behalf any releases or other documents that may be required in order to obtain this information.

(c) Consent to the disclosure of this information.

(If you want to limit the authority of your agent to receive and disclose information relating to your health, you must state the limitations in paragraph 4 ("Statement of Desires, Special Provisions, and Limitations") above.)

6. SIGNING DOCUMENTS, WAIVERS, AND RELEASES. Where necessary to implement the health care decisions that my agent is authorized by this document to make, my agent has the power and authority to execute on my behalf all of the following:

(a) Documents titled or purporting to be a "Refusal to Permit Treatment" and "Leaving Hospital Against Medical Advice."

(b) Any necessary waiver or release form, liability required by a hospital or physician.

7. AUTOPSY; ANATOMICAL GIFTS; DISPOSITION OF REMAINS. Subject to any limitations in this document, my agent has the power and authority to do all of the following:

(a) Authorize an autopsy under Section 7113 of the Health and Safety Code.

(b) Make a disposition of a part or parts of my body under the Uniform Anatomical Gift Act (Chapter 3.5 (commencing with Section 7150) of Part 1 of Davidson 7 of the Health and Safety Code).

(c) Direct the disposition of my remains under Section 7100 of the Health and Safety Code.

(If you want to limit the authority of your agent to consent to an autopsy, make an anatomical gift, or direct the disposition of your remains, you must state the limitations in paragraph 4 ("Statements of Desires, Special Provisions, and Limitations") above.)

8. DURATION
(Unless you specify otherwise in the space below, this power of attorney will exist for an indefinite period of time.)

This durable power of attorney for health care expires on _____
_____. (Fill in this space
ONLY if you want to limit the duration of this power of attorney.)

9. DESIGNATION OF ALTERNATE AGENTS.
(You are not required to designate any alternate agents but you may do so. Any alternate agent you designate will be able to make the same health care decisions as the agent you designated in paragraph 1, above, in the event that agent is unable or ineligible to act as your agent. If the agent you designated is your spouse, he or she becomes ineligible to act as your agent if your marriage is dissolved.)

If the person designated as my agent in paragraph 1 is not available or becomes ineligible to act as my agent to make a health care decision for me or loses the mental capacity to make health care decisions for me, or if I revoke that person's appointment or authority to act as my agent to make health care decisions for me, then I designate and appoint the following persons to serve as my agent to make health care decisions for me as authorized in this document, such persons to serve in the order listed below:

First Alternate Agent:

Second Alternate Agent:

Third Alternate Agent:

10. NOMINATION OF CONSERVATOR OF PERSON.
(A conservator of the person may be appointed for you if a court decides that one should be appointed. The conservator is responsible for your physical care, which under some circumstances includes making health care decisions for you. You are not required to nominate a conservator but you may do so. The court will appoint the person you nominate unless that would be contrary to your best interests. You may, but are not required to, nominate as your conservator the same person you named in paragraph 1 as your health care agent. You can nominate an individual as your conservator by completing the space below.)

If a conservator of the person is to be appointed for me. I nominate _____to serve as a conservator of the person.

11. PRIOR DESIGNATIONS REVOKED. I revoke any prior durable power of attorney for health care.

DATE AND SIGNATURE OF PRINCIPAL
(YOU MUST DATE AND SIGN THIS POWER OF ATTORNEY)

I sign my name to this Statutory Form Durable Power of Attorney for Health Care on:

_____ at_____, _____California_____
(Date)   (City)   (State)

_____

(THIS POWER OF ATTORNEY WILL NOT BE VALID UNLESS IT IS SIGNED BY TWO QUALIFIED WITNESSES WHO ARE PRESENT WHEN YOU SIGN OR ACKNOWLEDGE YOUR SIGNATURE. IF YOU HAVE ATTACHED ANY ADDITIONAL PAGES TO THIS FORM, YOU MUST DATE AND SIGN EACH OF THE ADDITIONAL PAGES AT THE SAME TIME YOU DATE AND SIGN THIS POWER OF ATTORNEY.)

STATEMENT OF WITNESSES

(This document must be witnessed by two qualified adult witnesses. None of the following may be sued as a witness: (1) a person you designate as your agent or alternate agent, (2) a health care provider, (3) an employee of a health care provider, (4) the operator of a community care facility, (5) an employee of an operator of a community care facility. At least one of the witnesses must make the additional declaration set out following the place where the witnesses sign.

READ CAREFULLY BEFORE SIGNING. (You can sign as a witness only if you personally know the principal or the identity of the principal is proved to you by convincing evidence.)
(To have convincing evidence of the identity of the principal, you must be presented with and reasonable rely on any one or more of the following:

(1)   An identification card or driver's license issued by the California Department of Motor Vehicles that is current or has been issued within five years.

(2)   A passport issued by the Department of State of the United States that is current or has been issued within five years.

(3)   Any of the following documents if the document is current or has been issued within five years and contains a photograph and description of the person named on it, is signed by the person, and bears a serial or other identifying number:

Safeguard Your Hard-Earned Savings

(a)   A passport issued by a foreign government that has been stamped by the United States Immigration and Naturalization Service.

(b)   A driver's license issued by a state other than California or by a Canadian or Mexican public agency authorized to issue driver's license.

(c)   An identification care issued by a state other than California.

(d)   An identification card issued by any branch of the armed forces of the United States.)

(Other kinds of proof of identity are not allowed.)

I declare under penalty of perjury under the laws of California that the person who signed or acknowledged this document is personally known to me (or proved to me on the basis of convincing evidence) to be the principal, that the principal signed or acknowledged this durable power of attorney in my presence, that the principal appears to be of sound mind and under no duress, fraud, or undue influence, that I am not the person appointed as attorney in fact by this document, and that I am not a health care provider, an employee of a health care provider, the operator of a community care facility, nor an employee of an operator of a community care facility.

Signature: _____   Address: _____

Witness 1

Date:

Signature: _____   Address: _____

Witness 2

Date:

(AT LEAST ONE OF THE ABOVE WITNESSES MUST ALSO SIGN THE FOLLOWING DECLARATION.)

I further declare under penalty of perjury under the laws of California that I am not related to the principal by blood, marriage, or adoption, and, to the best of my knowledge, I am not entitled to any part of the estate of the principal upon the death of the principal under a will now existing or by operation of law.

_____   _____

Witness 1   Witness 2

STATEMENT OF PATIENT ADVOCATE OR OMBUDSMAN

If you are a patient in a skilled nursing facility, one of the witnesses must be a patient advocate or ombudsman. The following statement is required only if you are a patient in a skilled nursing facility - a health care facility that provides the following basic services: skilled nursing care and supportive care to patients whose primary need is for availability of skilled nursing care on an extended basis. The patient advocate or ombudsman must sign both parts of the "Statement of Witness" above AND must also sign the following statement.

I further declare under penalty of perjury under the laws of California that I am a patient advocate or ombudsman as designated by the State Department of Aging and that I am serving as a witness as required by subdivision (f) of Section 2432 of the Civil Code.

_____

Signature

Appendix 3

Directory of Area Agencies on Aging

Each state has its own laws and regulations governing all types of insurance. The Area Agencies on Aging, listed in the right column, are responsible for coordinating services for older Americans. The left column lists telephone number(s) to call for insurance counseling services. Calls to an 800 number listed in this directory are free when made within the respective state.

Insurance counseling	*Area Agencies on Aging*
Alabama 800-243-5463	Commission on Aging 770 Washington Ave., Suite 470 Montgomery, AL 36130 P.O. Box 301851 800-243-5463 205-242-5743
Alaska 800-478-6065 907-562-7249	Older Alaskans Commission P.O. Box 110209 Juneau, AK 99811-0209 907-465-3250
Arizona 800-432-4040	Dept. of Economic Security Aging & Adult Administration 1789 W. Jefferson St. Phoenix, AZ 85007 602-542-4446

Arkansas
800-852-5494
501-686-2940

Division of Aging
and Adult Services
1417 Donaghey Plaza S.
P.O. Box 1437
Slot 1412
Little Rock, AR 72203-1437
501-682-2441

California
800-927-4357
916-323-7315

Department of Aging
1600 K St.
Sacramento, CA 95814
916-322-3887

Colorado
303-894-7499,
ext. 356

Aging and Adult Services
Dept. of Social Services
1575 Sherman St., 4th Fl.
Denver, CO 80203-1714
303-866-3851

Connecticut
800-443-9946

Elderly Services Division
175 Main St.
Hartford, CT 06106
1-800-443-9946
203-566-7772

Delaware
800-336-9500

Division of Aging
Dept. of Health & Social Services
1901 N. DuPont Hwy.
2nd Fl. Annex Admin.
New Castle, DE 19720
302-577-4791

District of Columbia
202-994-7463

Office on Aging
441 4th St. NW, 9th Fl.
Washington, DC 20001
202-724-5626
202-724-5622

Florida
904-922-2073

Department of Elder Affairs
1317 Winewood Blvd.
Building 1, Room 317
Tallahassee, FL 32399-0700
904-922-5297

Georgia
800-669-8387

Division of Aging Services
Dept. of Human Resources
2 Peachtree St. NW
Atlanta, GA 30303
404-657-5258

Hawaii
808-586-0100

Executive Office on Aging
335 Merchant St., Room 241
Honolulu, HI 96813
808-586-0100

Idaho
800-247-4422

Office on Aging
Statehouse, Room 108
Boise, ID 83720

Illinois
800-252-8966

Department on Aging
421 E. Capitol Ave.
Springfield, IL 62701
217-785-3356

Indiana
800-452-4800

Div. of Aging & Home Services
402 W. Washington St.
P.O. Box 7083
Indianapolis, IN 46207-7083
800-545-7763
317-232-7020

Iowa
515-281-5705

Dept. of Elder Affairs
Jewett Bldg., Suite 236
914 Grand Ave.
Des Moines, IA 50309
515-281-5187

Kansas
800-432-3535

Department on Aging
150-S. Docking State Office Bldg.
915 SW Harrison
Topeka, KS 66612-1500
913-296-4986

Kentucky
800-372-2991

Division of Aging Services
Cabinet for Human Resources
275 E. Main St., 5th Fl. West
Frankfort, KY 40621
502-564-6930

Louisiana
800-259-5301
504-342-5301

Governor's Office of
    Elderly Affairs
4550 N. Boulevard
P.O. Box 80374
Baton Rouge, LA 70896-0374
504-925-1700

Maine
800-750-5353
207-624-5335

Bureau of Elder and Adult Services
State House, Station 11
Augusta, ME 04333
207-624-5335

Maryland
800-243-3425

Office on Aging
301 W. Preston St., Room 1004
Baltimore, MD 21201
410-225-1102

Massachusetts
800-882-2003
617-727-7750

Executive Office of Elder Affairs
1 Ashburton Place, 5th Fl.
Boston, MA 02108
617-727-7750

Michigan
517-373-8230

Office of Services to the Aging
611 W. Ottawa St., Box 30026
Lansing, MI 48909
517-373-8230

Minnesota
800-882-6262

Board on Aging
Human Services Bldg., 4th Fl.
444 Lafayette Road
St. Paul, MN 55155-3843
612-296-2770

Mississippi
800-948-3090

Div. of Aging & Adult Services
750 N. State St.
Jackson, MS 39202
800-948-3090
601-359-4929

Missouri
800-390-3330

Division of Aging
Dept. of Social Services
Box 1337, 615 Howerton Court
Jefferson City, MO 65102-1337
314-751-3082

Montana
800-332-2272

Office on Aging
48 N. Last Chance Gulch
P.O. Box 8005
Helena, MT 59620
800-332-2272
406-444-5900

Nebraska
402-471-4506

Department of Aging
State Office Building
301 Centennial Mall S.
Lincoln, NE 68509-5044
402-471-2306

Nevada
702-367-1218
800-307-4444

Dept. of Human Resources
Division of Aging Services
340 N. 11th St.
Suite 114
Las Vegas, NV 89101
702-486-3545

New Hampshire
603-271-4642

Dept. of Health & Human Services
Div. of Elderly & Adult Services
State Office Park South
115 Pleasant St.
Annex Building No. 1
Concord, NH 03301
603-271-4680

New Jersey
800-792-8820

Dept. of Community Affairs
Division on Aging
S. Broad and Front streets
CN 807
Trenton, NJ 08625-0807
800-792-8820
609-984-3951

New Mexico
800-432-2080

State Agency on Aging
La Villa Rivera Bldg.
224 E. Palace Ave.
Santa Fe, NM 87501
800-432-2080
505-827-7640

New York
800-333-4114

State Office for the Aging
2 Empire State Plaza
Albany, NY 12223-0001
800-342-9871
518-474-5731

North Carolina
800-443-9354

Division of Aging
693 Palmer Drive, Caller Box 29531
Raleigh, NC 27626-0531
919-733-3983

North Dakota
800-247-0560

Dept. of Human Services
Aging Services Division
P.O. Box 7070
Bismarck, ND 58507-7070
701-224-2577

Ohio
800-686-1578

Department of Aging
50 W. Broad St., 9th Fl.
Columbus, OH 43266-0501
615-466-1221
800-282-1206

Oklahoma
405-521-6628

Dept. of Human Services
Aging Services Division
312 NE 28th St.
Oklahoma City, OK 73125
405-521-2327

Oregon
800-722-4134

Dept. of Human Resources
Senior & Disabled Services Div.
500 Summer St. NE, 2nd Fl.
Salem, OR 97310-1015
503-378-4728

Pennsylvania
717-783-8975

Department of Aging
400 Market St., State Office Bldg.
Harrisburg, PA 17101
717-783-1550

Rhode Island
800-322-2880

Dept. of Elderly Affairs
160 Pine Street
Providence, RI 02903
401-277-2858

South Carolina
800-868-9095

Division on Aging
202 Arbor Lake Drive
Suite 301
Columbia, SC 29223-4554
803-737-7500

South Dakota
605-773-3656

Office of Adult Services & Aging
700 Governors Drive
Pierre, SD 57501-2291
605-773-3656

Tennessee
800-525-2816

Commission on Aging
706 Church St.
Suite 201
Nashville, TN 37243-0860
615-741-2056

Texas
800-252-3439

Department on Aging
P.O. Box 12786 (787711)
1949 IH 35 S.
Austin, TX 78741
512-444-2727
800-252-9240

Utah
801-538-3910

Div. of Aging and Adult Services
120 North 200 West
P.O. Box 45500
Salt Lake City, UT 84145-0500
801-538-3910

Vermont
800-642-5119

Department of Aging & Disabilities
Waterbury Complex
103 S. Main Street
Waterbury, VT 05671-2301
802-241-2400

Virginia
800-552-4464

Department for the Aging
700 Centre, 10th Fl.
700 E. Franklin St.
Richmond, VA 23219-2327
800-552-4464
804-225-2271

Washington
800-397-4422

Aging & Adult Services Admin.
Dept. of Social & Health Services
P.O. Box 45050
Olympia, WA 98504-5050
206-586-3768

West Virginia
304-558-3317

Commission on Aging
State Capitol Complex
Holly Grove
1900 Kanawha Blvd. E.
Charleston, WV 25305-0160
304-558-3317

Wisconsin
800-242-1060

Board on Aging and Long Term Care
214 N. Hamilton St.
Madison, WI 53703
608-266-8944
800-242-1060

Wyoming
800-438-5768

Division on Aging
Hathaway Building
2300 Capitol Ave.
Room 139
Cheyenne, WY 82002
800-442-2766
307-777-7986

American Samoa

Territorial Administration on Aging
Government of American Samoa
Pago Pago, AS 96799
684-633-1252

**Commonwealth of the
Northern Mariana Islands**

Department of Community and
Cultural Affairs Civic Center
Commonwealth of the
    Northern Mariana Islands
Saipan, CM 96950
607-234-6011

**Federated States
of Micronesia**

State Agency on Aging
Office of Health Services
Federated States of Micronesia
Ponape, E.C.I. 96941

Guam

Division of Senior Citizens
Dept. of Public Health and
    Social Services
P.O. Box 2816
Agaña, Guam 96910
011 (671) 734-4361

Palau

State Agency on Aging
Dept. of Social Services
Republic of Palau
Koror, Palau 96940

Puerto Rico
809-721-5710

Governor's Office of
Elderly Affairs
Gericulture Commission
Box 11398
Santurce, PR 00910
809-722-2429

**Republic of the
Marshall Islands**

State Agency on Aging
Dept. of Social Services
Republic of the Marshall Islands
Marjuro, Marshall Islands 96960

Virgin Islands
809-774-2991

Senior Citizen Affairs Div.
Dept. of Human Services
19 Estate Diamond
Fredericksted
St. Croix, VI 00840
809-772-0930

Appendix 4

State long-term care ombudsman programs

California

California Ombudsman Program
Department of Aging
1600 K St.
Sacramento, CA 95814
916-323-6681

Florida

State Long-Term Care Ombudsman
    Council
Office of the Governor Carlton Bldg.
501 S. Calhoun St.
Tallahassee, FL 32399-0001

Georgia

Department of H.R., Office of Aging
2 Peachtree St. NW, 18th Fl.
Atlanta, GA 30303
404-894-5336

Illinois

Department of Aging
421 E. Capitol, 1st Fl.
Springfield, IL 62701
217-785-2870

Indiana

Family and Social Services Admin.
Division of Disability, Aging and
    Rehabilitative Services—Bureau
    of Aging/In-Home Services
P.O. Box 7083
Indianapolis, IN 46207-7083
317-232-7134

Iowa

Long-Term Care
    Advocate/Ombudsman
Department of Elder Affairs
236 Jewett Building—914 Grand Ave.
Des Moines, IA 50309
515-281-5187

Kansas

Department on Aging
Docking State Office Building
Suite 150
915 SW Harrison
Topeka, KS 66612
913-296-4986

Louisiana

Governor's Office of Elderly Affairs
P.O. Box 80374
Baton Rouge, LA 70898-0374
504-925-1700

Massachusetts

Long-Term Care Ombudsman
Office of Elder Affairs
1 Ashburton Place
5th Fl.
Boston, MA 02108
617-727-7750

Michigan

Citizens for Better Care
416 N. Homer St.
Suite 101
Lansing, MI 48912-4716
517-336-6753

Minnesota

Minnesota Board on Aging and
Office of the Ombudsman for
Older Minnesotans
444 Lafayette Road
St. Paul, MN 55155-3843
612-296-2770

Missouri

Division of Aging
Long-Term Care Ombudsman
1615 Howerton Court
P.O. Box 1337
Jefferson City, MO 65102
314-751-3082

New Jersey

Office of the Ombudsman for the
Institutionalized Elderly
101 S. Broad and Front streets
CN 808
Trenton, NJ 08625-0808
609-292-8016

New York

Office for the Aging
Long-Term Care Ombudsman Program
Empire State Plaza, 2nd Fl., Bldg. 2
Albany, NY 12223
518-474-5731

Ohio

Department of Aging
Long-Term Care Ombudsman Office
50 W. Broad Street, 8th Fl.
Columbus, OH 43215
614-466-1221

Oklahoma

Department. of Human Services,
Aging Services Division
312 NE 28th St.
Oklahoma City, OK 73108
405-521-2327

Pennsylvania

Department of Aging—Office of the
State Long-Term Care Ombudsman
231 State St.
Harrisburg, PA 1901-1195
717-783-7247

Tennessee

Commission on Aging
Andrew Jackson Building, 9th Fl.
Nashville, TN 37243-0860
615-741-2056

Texas

Dept. on Aging, Elder Rights Div.
P.O. Box 12786
Austin, TX 78711
512-444-2727

Wisconsin

Bureau on Aging and Long-Term Care
214 N. Hamilton St.
Madison, WI 53703
608-266-8945

Index

A

Activities of daily living
   (ADL), 57, 62, 76, 93
Adult day care, 15, 79
Advanced directives, 142-144
Advocacy, for nursing home
   patients, 145-146
"Aging American, Trends and
   Projections," 15
Aid to Families with Dependent
   Children, 41
Alzheimer's disease, 15, 17, 62, 76,
   79-80, 100, 133
A.M. Best, 44, 78
American Association of Retired
   Persons (AARP), 60
Americans with Disabilities Act
   (ADA), 20-23
Annual income, 14
Annuities, 107-111, 126-127
Area Agency on Aging, 63, 94, 102,
   132, 145-146
Asset-protection tools, 115
Assets, 101, 103-111, 137-138
   countable, 35
   noncountable, 36
   transferring, 118-122, 126
Assisted living, 53-55, 63
Assured care, 82-83
Average Indexed Monthly Earnings
   (AIME), 29

B

Beneficiary, 111
Benefit state, 102
   for children, 28-29
   for disabled widow, 29
   for worker's family, 28
   insurance, 77-80
   Social Security, 26-31
Blindness, 28

C

Capital gains tax, 54
Care,
   adult day, 15, 79
   assured, 82-83
   convalescent, 16-17
   custodial, 15, 62, 79
   facilities, 132-133
   home health, 79
   intermediate, 15, 62, 79
   long-term, 15-17
   respite, 15, 79
   skilled, 62, 79
Caregivers, tasks performed
   by, 59-60
Children, benefits for, 28-29
Community Spousal Resource
   Allowance (CSRA), 103, 109, 125
Compounding inflation rider, 44-45

Was the information you just read important to you?

Do you feel you learned from this valuable material?

Would you like to learn more?

If you answered yes to one or more of the above questions, you need to subscribe to *Mature American*.

Mature American is a newsletter that will keep you one step ahead of the rapidly changing times. In an easy-to-read format, you will get detailed information on financial, health and consumer topics designed for Americans who are either retired or planning for retirement.

Subscribe today by calling the toll-free hotline at 1-800-728-8901 with your credit card ready, or send a check made payable to:

> *Mature American*
> 17065 Via Del Campo, Suite 101
> San Diego, CA 92127

There is a limited number of both *Complete Guide to Investing in Mutual Funds* and *Senior Savvy*. To ensure you receive your FREE GIFT—Act today!